For Us, What Music?

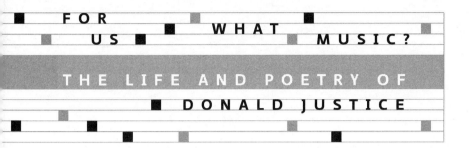

FOR US WHAT MUSIC?
THE LIFE AND POETRY OF DONALD JUSTICE

by Jerry Harp

To Father John Kavanaugh,
with admiration!

Jerry Harp
Portland, OR
14 Jan. 2011

University
of Iowa Press
Iowa City

University of Iowa Press, Iowa City 52242
Copyright © 2010 by the University of Iowa Press
www.uiowapress.org
Printed in the United States of America

Design by Omega Clay

Part of the introduction is taken from Jerry Harp, "Fidelities
to Form: On Donald Justice's *Oblivion: On Writers and Writing,*" *Iowa Review* 29.3 (Winter 1999): 167–72. Part of chapter 4
was presented as part of a panel on Donald Justice, chaired by
Robert Dana, at the 2005 conference of the Associated Writing Programs, Vancouver BC. Poetry from *Collected Poems* by
Donald Justice, © 2004 by Donald Justice, used by permission
of Alfred A. Knopf, a division of Random House, Inc.

The University of Iowa Press is a member of Green Press
Initiative and is committed to preserving natural resources.

Printed on acid-free paper

Library of Congress Cataloging-in-Publication Data
For us, what music?: the life and poetry of Donald Justice / by
Jerry Harp.
    p. cm.
Includes bibliographical references and index.
ISBN-13: 978-1-58729-911-7 (pbk.)
ISBN-10: 1-58729-911-9 (pbk.)
ISBN-13: 978-1-58729-944-5 (e-book)
ISBN-10: 1-58729-944-5 (e-book)
1. Justice, Donald Rodney, 1925–2004—Criticism and inter-
pretation. 2. Justice, Donald Rodney, 1925–2004—Aesthetics.
I. Title. II. Title: Life and poetry of Donald Justice.
PS3519.U825Z656 2010
811'.54—dc22   2010011576

CONTENTS

ACKNOWLEDGMENTS

I owe thanks to more people than I can name. For now it must suffice to mention the help of Marvin Bell, Peg Dana, Rocco DiLorenzo, Doug Erickson, Kurt Fosso, David Hamilton, Jeff Hamilton, Susan Kirschner, Paul Merchant, Robert Mezey, Will Pritchard, Michael Smolinsky, Jason Sommer, Richard Stern, and Rishona Zimring.

I express my gratitude to the following: the staff of Special Collections at the University of Iowa Library; Robert Dana for his conversation and assistance, as well as for opening to me his personal archive; William Logan for the hours he spent commenting on the first chapter; Mary Szybist for her endless patience, years of conversation, and critical commentary on the entire book; Molly Bellman and Ancil Nance for their hospitality and the use of their study space; and Jessie Dolch for her excellent work copyediting the manuscript. This book has benefited immeasurably from the help of all of these people and many others. Whatever faults remain are entirely my own.

I extend a special thanks to Jean Ross Justice, whose many hours of conversation and endless e-mails have allowed this book to be much more deeply informed than it otherwise could have been. I dedicate this book to her.

With the appearance of Donald Justice's *Collected Poems* (2004), the sheer diversity of his achievement came into full view. As Willard Spiegelman noted in his review, Justice was "as fluid and open to new gestures as [Robert] Lowell and [John] Ashbery" (158). The comparison to Ashbery may surprise some readers, but I hope to show that Justice should be considered among the great experimental poets of the latter half of the twentieth century. As Charles Simic put it, "Justice was a most unusual kind of poet"—"both a formalist and a committed modernist at a time when these two aesthetics seemed incompatible" (225). Much of what made these aesthetics compatible for Justice was his conviction that literary tradition remains alive by being altered. In this regard he was a poet such as T. S. Eliot describes in "Tradition and the Individual Talent"—one who both struggles to do something that has never been done before and also knows that making something new means engaging with the past.

When I was Justice's student in the Program in Creative Writing at the University of Florida in the fall of 1989, he set out a program of study for us in the first class session; he was calm and gentlemanly, almost old-world in manner. He said that he would give us no assignments because, as we had come to the writing program, he assumed that we would be reading and writing all the time. We should read poetry in English from all centuries. We should read the poetry of other languages (in the original if possible—if not, then in translation) from at least the past two centuries. He gave us a long handout exemplifying an array of verse forms. Throughout the semester he dropped deceptively simple words of advice into our discussion. To this day, much of what he said is still unfolding itself to me. I have heard others among his former students say much the same.

Years later, after Justice retired and he and his wife, Jean, moved back to Iowa City, I decided to write this book. I was living in Iowa City as well, and after I found out that Don approved of the idea, I made a habit of taking along note cards when I visited with him and Jean. My wife, Mary, and I would sit in their living room where the windows, beside which sat a baby grand piano, gave onto the Iowa River. Art books occupied the shelves in the corner. Often, books and recent literary magazines lay spread out on the coffee table. Much of the biographical information in this book comes from our conversations with Don and Jean over the years.

The first chapter provides a biographical overview up to the publication of Justice's first full-length volume of poems, *The Summer Anniversaries* (1960). Thereafter, the chapters focus primarily on his work, though a biographical narrative runs through the book, providing part of the context for understanding the poems. Except for chapters 1 and 6, each chapter considers the work in order of book publication. Thus, chapter 2 focuses on *The Summer Anniversaries* and the importance of the story of the expulsion from Eden, the myth of the fall from original unity to the complexities of history. This myth helps to make sense of the reflective nostalgias of Justice's poems, which look with fondness to images of a lost world that the poems intimate is inaccessible and most likely never really existed. Chapter 3 takes up *Night Light* (1967) and the complications of human identity and self-alienation, both of which can be precarious though they also allow the human person flexibility and creativity. Distance from oneself allows room for creative action. Important here also is the image of the double agent; for the self-aware, complex, and self-alienated person becomes a kind of double agent in everyday life. Chapter 4 focuses on *Departures* (1973) and Justice's experiments with chance methods, which he took up after forming a friendship with John Cage. These methods allowed Justice to develop in new directions the artistic depersonalization to which he was committed. Chapter 5 treats Justice's return to experiments with meter in *The Sunset Maker* (1987), along with the new poems that appeared in *New and Selected Poems* (1995), *Orpheus Hesitated beside the Black River* (1998), and *Collected Poems* (2004). This chapter also returns to the issue of tradition and how engagement with the formal disciplines of art help one to understand the world. Chapter 6 then considers the Orphic strain in Justice's entire career. In alliance with the mythic poet, many of Justice's poems gesture toward a community that includes the living and the dead.

Throughout, this book emphasizes Justice's commitment to art, especially the art of poetry. For him, art was a way of life. It not only provided its own wealth of experiences worthy in themselves, but also allowed rich and nuanced ways of experiencing, understanding, and being in the world. As I hope this study shows, Justice's poetry provides and allows its reader the same.

For Us, What Music?

Donald Justice believed in art as a vocation. In "Oblivion: Variations on a Theme," he expressed this belief "in a language bearing overtones of the spiritual": "The vows may not be codified and published, but they are secretly known and one does take them. I am perfectly serious about this" (1998a, 52). The idea of vocation also occurs in his short story "Death, Night, Etc.," in which Taylor Smith, having given up the serious pursuit of music, says, "It's as though I'd fled a monastery, broken vows" (1998b, 75). For Justice, the monastic vows of art signaled a calling and lifelong commitment.

Although raised a Southern Baptist, he stopped believing in God early, but he believed deeply in art throughout his adult years (Justice 2001, 18). While in his devotion to form he might be considered a classicist—albeit a "postmodern classicist" for his commitment to "innovation and experiment"[1] as well as to form—he followed the Romantics in his applications of traditional religious language and categories to his poetry. He thus provides a latter-day example of the Romantics' "secularization of inherited theological ideas and ways of thinking" (Abrams 12). Although his comments on poetry do not bear the same grand overtones as the Romantics' desire to create a new world by the union of nature and the human mind (ibid., 21–29), his faith in art nevertheless constituted a way of finding meaning in human experience. Whereas the Romantics' language tended toward the prophetic, in the sense of divine disclosure and proclamation (see Rahner and Vorgrimler 383–84), Justice's tended toward the contemplative.

A somewhat more recent literary movement that provides a model for the transference of religious impulses and language to art is the French symbolism that Edmund Wilson (1–25) described as a further development of Romanticism. This style of devotion to literature had its effects on the English Pre-Raphaelites, but it remained very much a French movement, exemplified among Justice's influences by Rimbaud and Baudelaire. In describing the figures of this movement, Arthur Symons pointed out that for them literature "becomes itself a kind of religion, with all the duties and responsibilities of the sacred ritual" (10). Justice translated the language of these duties and responsibilities into a learned American vernacular. At the same time, he also realized that the metaphor of art as religious devotion had to be tempered. After his early formation, he did not mistake—at least not for long—art for life, or vice versa. "Art keeps long hours," as he put it in "On a Picture by Burchfield,"[2] but then so does life; both make their own demands, and much of Justice's early life was taken up with a struggle to synthesize the two. The devotion to art gave his life form and focus even as it brought complications.

In the opening poem of *The Summer Anniversaries*, the speaker announces, "Great Leo roared at my birth" ("Anniversaries," CP 5). Whether such a portent accompanied the birth of Donald Rodney Justice on August 12, 1925, the event was observed with due solemnity. As Jean Ross Justice recounts: "Donald's grandmother held him up to see the sunrise; this was reported later. It was a family with a sense of occasion" (1). Justice's parents, Mary Ethel (Cook) and Vasco Justice, had moved to Miami from south Georgia. His mother grew up in Boston, Georgia, and his father, though born in Pansy, Alabama (a hamlet that no longer exists), moved with his family to a farm near Tifton, Georgia. Their son recalled visiting this latter area as "a part of my summers growing up, not a part I really liked."[3] From early on Justice was a denizen of the city, albeit the rather quiet city that was the Miami of his childhood.

When Vasco was in the army during World War I, he and Mary Ethel began to correspond. They had never met, but a mutual friend supplied her with the young man's name. Following the war, and after Vasco found work in Miami as a carpenter, they married. He was able to make a good living during the days of Miami's land boom, which lasted from 1915 to 1925. This period of sometimes frenzied land speculation and burgeoning construction ended after the hurricane of September 17–18, 1926. Florida's economy was slow to recover; as one study of this period puts it, "Depression came to Florida almost four years before it appeared in the national economy" (Frazer and Guthrie 153–54). When Donald was about four years old, he found his mother packing a suitcase and asked what she was doing. She explained that his father was going to Texas to look for work. As luck would have it, however, that very day Vasco came home and announced that he had found a job doing maintenance and repair work on Biscayne Bay. The job carried the family through the Depression.[4]

Much later Justice said that he had come to think of his childhood as a happy one, though he had not always thought of it that way (2001, 20). Jean Justice conjectures that part of what made Donald's childhood seem to him an enchanted realm were the attentions of his mother, as exemplified in the many photographs that she took of her only child.[5] For example, there is one of young Donald dressed as the groom in a "Tom Thumb Wedding," an event popular in the 1930s in which children played the roles of a wedding party. On some photographs she wrote captions from the boy's point of view: "Me and my birthday cake," "Me and my dog," and (on a photograph of Donald eating watermelon) "Guess what I'm eating." Of these early years, Justice recalled, "I was an only child, and as such I was spoiled, especially by my mother, who gave me the sense early on that what I did I could and should do well, the sense also that we were as good as anyone and ought *never* to forget that" (2001, 20).

Jean also believes that another enchantment of Donald's childhood was the milieu of Miami in the 1920s and 1930s, when it was a much smaller city than now, taken up with a romantic notion of constructing ideal suburban spaces with arched entrances and other such accoutrements. Recall the ending of Justice's poem "Childhood":

> And sometimes,
> Where the city halts, the cracked sidewalks
> Lead to a coral archway still spanning
> The entrance to some wilderness of palmetto—
>
> Forlorn suburbs, but with golden names! (CP 191)

This poem, dedicated "to the poets of a mythical childhood: Wordsworth, Rimbaud, Rilke, Hart Crane, Alberti," presents a self-consciously mythic version of Justice's past. It calls attention to its gestures of idealization even as it questions them with details of "cracked sidewalks" and "Forlorn suburbs." One way that the poem signals its self-consciousness is by the theatrical opening, which stages the poem as a kind of play:

> TIME: *the thirties*
> PLACE: *Miami, Florida*

> Once more beneath my thumb the globe turns—
> And doomed republics pass in a blur of colors . . . (CP 189)

The staging of time and location emphasizes that this is a work of artifice, a remaking of the past on the writer's terms. The "doomed republics" beneath the speaker's thumb signal a major preoccupation of Justice's work—the attempt to preserve a fading past; in this poem, the speaker's childhood is itself a doomed republic. The regime, the state of affairs of this childhood, was doomed from the start; the ellipsis at the end of the second line blends the colors of the present moment with those recollected from the past as the speaker recalls his childhood, along with its doom, not without a certain pleasure. The story that emerges is one that remains prominent through much of Justice's writing: the loss of an Edenic space, along with the sorrows and pleasures of such a loss, which is the very condition of realizing the past. One must have lost the past to know it in a way that was not possible when one was there. It is surely no accident that it was only in his later years that Justice came to think of his childhood as a happy one. The golden names shimmer only in retrospect. They also shimmer because they are set in the midst of forlorn suburbs. One can catch a glimpse of the world as idealized and somehow whole precisely because it is broken, like the cracked sidewalks, from the start. The fragment enables the imagination to build its myth.

The Justices did well in the less-than-ideal world. Although they were not wealthy, they could afford the piano lessons that Donald began at age five. He recalled in his brief memoir "Piano Lessons: Notes on a Provincial Culture": "A piano lesson in those days cost fifty cents and lasted for half an hour. At that price my parents, though far from well off, were able to afford a weekly lesson for me all through the depression years" (1987, 33). This student of the piano also proved to be a fine student of the general curriculum at Allapattah Elementary School, where he was double-promoted. Then in the summer of 1935, he was diagnosed with the osteomyelitis (an infectious bone disease) that caused him to miss a year of school. But the forced absence did not stop his informal education, for he read voraciously during his convalescence; Twain, Poe, Dreiser, *The Last of the Mohicans*, and *The Brothers Karamazov* were some of the "famous books" and authors that he thought "one ought to read" (2001, 19). When he was in eleventh grade, it was reading William Cullen Bryant's "Inscription for the Entrance to a Wood" that "converted" him to a devotion to poetry (CS 172).

An anecdote from the time of Justice's convalescence recalls a moment of realization that could have come from one of his poems. He was lying in bed one evening when he realized that the hammering he had been hearing was his father building a house nearby, a job that the elder Justice accomplished almost single-handedly, after the hours of his regular job, to make money for his son's medical expenses (Justice 2001, 18). The anecdote calls to mind the ethic of hard work that formed an intimate part of Justice's early experience, as it also registers a sense of separation from the everyday world proceeding around him. In "Anniversaries" (CP 5) Justice captures something of this feeling of separation:

At ten there came an hour
When, waking out of ether
Into an autumn weather
Inexpressibly dear,
I was wheeled superb in a chair
Past vacant lots in bloom
With goldenrod and with broom,
In secret proud of the scar
Dividing me from life,
Which I could admire like one
Come down from Mars or the moon,
Standing a little off.

In retrospect the scar becomes the sign, inscribed on the boy's body, of an artistic calling demanding that one stand "a little off," to be divided "from life" to the extent that allows him to view human experience, including his own, with what has traditionally been called aesthetic distance. The narrator of Justice's short story "Death, Night, Etc." says of Eugene Bestor (the fictitious composer who also figures in Justice's poem "The Sunset Maker"), "He seemed somehow to be standing just a little apart from those he was with, even from Florence and me; not consciously and meaning nothing by it, I am sure" (1998b, 64). It may be that in Justice's conception of an artistic life, it is necessary to stand a little apart this way—not with the kind of "haughtiness toward life" (ibid., 56) that Arthur Symons attributes to the symbolist poet Villiers, but rather with the kind of distance that T. S. Eliot described in "Tradition and the Individual Talent" as a "continual extinction of personality" (1960, 7). Because the "emotion of art is impersonal" (ibid., 11), one must stand a little apart even from oneself.

Justice attended Andrew Jackson High School in Miami, playing clarinet in the school band and the orchestra. In the fall of 1941, he moved to Miami Senior High, where he graduated in spring 1942. His friend Laurence Donovan recalled meeting him "through mutual friends, some time in my high-school days" (CS 103). Donovan also recalled John Lenox, whom Justice met in middle school and whose dedication to music he fondly recalled.[6] The *Miami Herald* dated May 1, 1943, carries a story about Lenox, "one of the *Herald's* carrier boys," taking "musical honors." Having graduated from Miami Senior High at age sixteen, Lenox won a full scholarship to study bassoon at the Eastman School of Music in Rochester, New York. The story explains that the "young musician will earn the rest of his expenses during the summer with his carrier route. He distributes 400 papers daily." Lenox also bought his bassoon, which cost five hundred dollars, with money that he earned as a newspaper carrier. Donovan paid tribute to Lenox as a "type of American now disappearing from the scene" (CS 109). In his poem "In Memory of My Friend, the Bassoonist, John Lenox" (CP 211–12), Justice also described the musician, in affectionately ironic terms, as

> the best
> Contrabassoonist south
> Of Washington, D.C.—
> The only one.

He goes on to describe Lenox sitting "Lonely/ /In eminence" like "some lost island king." Perhaps something that these two notes of tribute hold in common, and which also may explain what Donovan meant by a "type of American now disappearing from the scene," is a conviction that a singular devotion to one's art, regardless of worldly success, is what leads to authentic eminence. Similar is Justice's tribute to Donovan himself, in his foreword to the latter's *Dog Island and Other Florida Poems* (2003), where he describes Donovan's "preferences and leanings" set against the "trends and fashions of the time and place," accounting for the "solitariness of his fame" (9). I suspect that by the latter phrase Justice means a fame limited to the few who shared his tastes and preferences. Although critical recognition caught up with Justice, he stayed true to his tastes and preferences as well.

Donovan also remembered Robert Boardman Vaughn—a rather elegant if self-destructive bohemian figure. As Donovan wrote, Vaughn, "whose gaunt, wild-eyed, apparitional figure I encountered first in my high-school days, and to whom among his teachers Don dedicated his book *The Sunset Maker*, was a dreamer and poet who followed his elusive muse through the Caribbean, producing little poetry but, as Don writes in 'Portrait with One Eye,' making his life a poem" (CS 106). Vaughn was never Justice's teacher in any formal sense, but Justice admired his fierce devotion to poetry and his taste in literature generally. They were friends until Vaughn's disappearance, despite what Donovan calls "Vaughn's frequent affronts" (ibid.) to Justice. Years later, Justice managed to procure some funding for Vaughn to attend the University of Iowa. Having sat through a presentation by Justice on Emily Dickinson, Vaughn approached his friend to tell him that it was the worst lecture he had ever heard. As Justice recalled decades later, "It was not a bad lecture." Vaughn left town and the university without telling his friend.[7]

Nevertheless, Justice wrote many poems paying fond tribute to this fellow devotee of poetry.

In fall 1942 Justice enrolled at the University of Miami, which he attended on a band scholarship. During his freshman year, he was invited to join the university writers' club, the Snarks, an "unprecedented honor for a freshman" (Jean Justice 7). He gained a reputation as the group aesthete, noted for his "modernist" or "obscure" writing style (Justice 2001, 27). One year the campus newspaper reported that he had "caused recent campus bewilderment by his play *Surrealist Police*" (quoted in Jean Justice 7). He also carried on a correspondence with George Marion O'Donnel, a "second-generation fugitive Agrarian from Vanderbilt" (Justice 2001, 26), who was teaching at the Alabama Polytechnic Institute. One of Justice's high school friends, a student in O'Donnel's freshman course, had shown his teacher some of Justice's poems, and O'Donnel invited the University of Miami freshman for a visit. Justice recalled, "I took the train up from Miami and there I was treated to talk about poems such as I had never heard before—Hardy, Blake, Dante, I remember—and in general treated like an adult" (ibid., 26). O'Donnel read and commented on the young poet's work, with an eye toward "what was lacking and what perhaps wasn't" (CS 175). As Justice also recalled of this visit, "Encouragement meant a great deal to me" (ibid., 175). Through O'Donnel's intervention Justice had his first national publication, in the February 1943 issue of *Mademoiselle*. The poem, titled "The Scarred Men, She," begins

> On what faint land on what sea
> Riding the cloud or riding the sun
> Beneath what tree under what shroud
> Sleeping on sand or sleeping on gun
> O where are they lurking for me.

Justice later commented that at this time he "hadn't really caught on to the meters yet."[8] Indeed, some of the lines stumble in their rhythms—an especially notable example follows those just quoted: "Behind what white hands behind what heart"—but much of the poem maintains its stately iambics with an admixture of anapestic and trochaic substitutions.

During his first year of college, Justice was selected to study musical composition under Carl Ruggles. Because he was a freshman, he had to take the course without credit. He later remarked that in studying under Ruggles, what "counted was the model he was in himself of the artist, the serious artist, one dedicated to the very highest ends" (2001, 24). Back when he was in high school, around age fifteen, Justice and his best friend wanted to compose music. Although Justice respected the music of the past, once he "heard The Rite of Spring on record," he was "eager for more of the present, though anything contemporary was hard to come by in those days" (ibid., 21). No doubt Ruggles, with his "modern dissonant style" (Ziffrin 60), was an excellent teacher for the young composer. Ruggles had begun teaching at the University of Miami, with a single course, in the spring of 1937. As he continued his work at the university, enrollment in his courses increased, though by Justice's freshman year (1942–43), enrollment was down again because of the war. Justice was one of only two students who received private lessons from Ruggles. In her biography of the composer, Marilyn J. Ziffrin provides further details: "As Justice remembered it, there was a long living room and dining room at one end of the house, and an alcove where Carl set up his easel. They had brought paintings from Arlington, and these were displayed on the walls around the house. There was also a small upright piano on which he and the students worked" (169). Justice later took up painting himself, and after his retirement from teaching, he also returned to musical composition. Some of his complex and dissonant pieces were publicly performed at the University of Iowa.

In fall 1944 Justice stopped, on his way to New York, at the University of North Carolina at Chapel Hill. In the library he saw a young man reading Louis Untermeyer's anthology *Modern British and American Poetry.* "Good stuff," Justice commented (CS 112). The young man was Richard Stern, with whom Justice struck up a correspondence that lasted more than half a century. Stern recalls that even though Justice "hated inherited class privilege" (ibid., 112), he was nevertheless an aristocrat of the world of poetry, the world of which Stern wanted to be a part. Stern is now known as a distinguished writer of fiction, though at the time he was writing poems. He sent some pieces that he was working on to Justice, who responded in a letter dated March 3, 1946:

> The two poems you sent me I will be honest about. I did not like them. Although nobody else could have written them, they were not original. You are trying to be Elizabethan, modern and Stern all at the same time. You should really be more stern about it. I realize this is bad criticism, not cutting to the heart of any matter, really nothing but a minor witticism, which is what too many critics of the New Yorker school repeat all their lives. What is really wrong with the poems is that they show lack of organization, no feeling for form (though I remember one was cast into a rough sort of sonnet, wasn't it?

there was still no <u>form</u> there), uncontrolled meter, now and then an obvious rhyme, and quite often a banal or borrowed image; furthermore, no suggestion of a complete world-picture was there, no moral structure behind or beneath the surface of the poems which would serve to give them meaning and life. Of course I am a fool if I expect to find such in only two poems. Nevertheless it is true that I would like to. Some good things in them, principally in a few phrases such as "the continent of things." But this entire paragraph is really rather superfluous because you must have known before you sent them how I would react, or at least what was really wrong and what was really right about them. They seemed hurried and probably were, though I have faith that you must on some things spend a great deal of time. At any rate, send me some more of your work and at least let me look at it. If you'd rather, I can keep my mouth closed about it.[9]

Quite striking about this early letter is the conviction and intellectual reach of the evaluation, along with the thorough self-awareness—as in the desire for a suggestion of a world picture to give "meaning and life" to the poems, even as the critic realizes that he is asking too much of only two pieces. As he intimates, however, such a desire will not dissipate, so the poet must somehow provide. The letter shows a complex understanding in its distinction between distinctiveness and originality, for verse can be both unmistakable in its authorship and quite derivative. The letter's call for a poetry that displays a "feeling for form," as well as discloses a sense of the world, shows a sophistication (Justice was only twenty years old when he wrote this letter) that indicates how seriously Justice already took the art of poetry. While this is not yet the voice of the adult man, it is witty, self-aware (even mildly self-mocking), sensitive to craft, and alert to matters of vision. Stern comments about this letter, "What intrigues me most now and, I imagine, moved me most at the time was the easy progression in his judgment from taste—or in this instance, distaste—to the high-minded, non-technical standards that underwrote it."[10]

During his undergraduate years, Justice spent a short time as a student at Chapel Hill, which he entered in 1944. He remained there several months, but because the university would not accept all of his University of Miami credits, and perhaps because of his limited funds, he returned to graduate from Miami (Jean Justice 8).

The only poet of national reputation whom Justice heard read during his undergraduate years was Robert Frost, who wintered in Miami (PS 78). Because Justice had become friends with Frost's grandson Prescott, he was able once or twice to have lunch with the elder poet. Justice never tried to draw

Frost out on matters of poetry, perhaps because he then favored Eliot. He recalled that Frost "did not care for Eliot or Eliot fans, though in my presence he was never anything but polite about it" (2001, 27). Although Justice never lost his taste for Eliot, he would later come to see Frost as the great American poet of the twentieth century.[11]

Because he had taken heavy course loads, Justice received his bachelor's degree in English in the spring of 1945. In the fall he moved to New York City. In an interview with Philip Hoy, he recalled this time: "I knocked about Greenwich Village for some months; I took a few odd jobs, and did some of the romantic things young would-be writers used to do—like hitchhiking and sleeping on subways. Not, of course, doing any writing" (2001, 27–28). Among his jobs were selling original designs by aspiring artists at a jewelry store and working as an assistant furniture mover.[12] He also put in a stint at *Mademoiselle* and worked a low-wage job for Paramount Pictures (Jean Justice 8). During part of his sojourn in the city, he lived with his friend Robert Vaughn. Jean Justice recalls that once "they fell out over a literary judgment—who was better than whom—and Bob said that *if that was what Don thought* he should move out. How much more serious about literature could anyone be?" (ibid., 9). Justice did indeed move out.

There is a photograph of him from this period, taken by Arthur Fellig, the tabloid photographer known as Weegee, in the basement apartment of the jazz trumpeter Frankie Newton (CS 174). As Edwin London wrote of Justice, "Don traveled in hipster music circles as a youth and was up-to-the-moment in Diz, Bud, and Bird" (ibid., 147). In the Weegee photograph, Justice sits on the floor, smoking, much taken by the moment—a portrait of the young artist, even if he is not doing any writing at the time. One also catches a glimpse in this photograph of the "tall, thin young man" who "wore his hair a trifle longer than was customary at the time, at least at the University of North Carolina" (Jean Justice 117).

Justice began graduate work at Chapel Hill in fall 1946. The early days of life as a graduate student were lonely for him, as he described in a letter to his friend Barbara Pearson:

> Did I tell you about all the sad young men here? As soon as classes are over for the day they stand in a long line for lunch and sit at tables by themselves; then go to the Student Union and lounge in the big stuffed chairs, turning the pages over of last year's Life's, not even having a partner with whom to play ping-pong. They go to the movies too, every afternoon, and maybe sit through it twice, not wanting to come out and stand in the long line for supper again, and sit at the lonely table all over again. I know; I'm one of them.[13]

The details sound common enough for a graduate student, but more was taking place in his life than this solitary wandering from class to student union to the movies. The letter describes also something of a crisis Justice was undergoing in his sense of himself as an artist:

> I've been reading a great deal of Southern literature the last few months, at last beginning to get the feel of a real tradition into which I may soon be able to fit. However, all of the self-confidence, that wonderful faith in my own high destiny I used to have at seventeen is broken into little pieces. There's a lot I could add to this, but it only be [sic] a silly little attempt at self-evaluation—things about a consciousness of guilt, a very real one too, that I seem to carry around with me like a shadow.

This fragmentation of self-confidence and faith in his destiny, which amounted to a fragmentation of his own identity, was related also to feeling too removed from life for the sake of an artistic ideal unrealizable in the everyday world:

> But I used to think to live for Art was great, which was a devilish perversion. A platitude I just made up—Art is only a part of Life. And to live Life for its sake has now become my perversion, into which I will of course try to fit a little Art too, but in proper ratio. So far, though, I can't seem to force my way into Life; been breathing the cold thin air on top of Mount Art for too long.

He would go on to find ways to integrate his life with his art (for example, by teaching the craft of poetry, to which he devoted himself), but in the meantime there was the practical matter of pursuing a degree in literature.

Arriving in his Chaucer course without a book, he asked to look on with a young woman named Jean Ross, who was sitting in the back row. She consented despite her reservations about associating herself with so unserious a student. She recalls referring to this thin young man as the "guy who's going to flunk out of graduate school" (CS 117). She herself came from quite a serious literary family. Her sister is the poet Eleanor Ross Taylor, who married the novelist and short fiction writer Peter Taylor in 1943. The Ross brothers published novels: James wrote *They Don't Dance Much* (1940), about a man who runs a roadhouse and whose moneymaking scheme leads to murder; Fred would win the Houghton Mifflin Fiction Prize for his novel *Jackson Mahaffey* (1951). Robert Vaughn alluded to the former title in a letter to Justice: "As Stanley would say, 'Man, the days are going by like the music played on a roller piano' and as Ross would say 'They Don't Dance Much.'"[14]

Not only did Justice not flunk out of graduate school, he began keeping regular company with the young woman whose Chaucer book he shared.

They attended an informal writers' group, called the Saucer Club, that met over coffee at a place called Danziger's (CS 127). The group included Richard Stern and the poet Edgar Bowers, who stated that "all of us enjoyed Don and Jean's being so intelligently and nicely in love" (ibid., 127). Donald began to co-write a play with Stern while they were at Chapel Hill (Izzo 10–12), though by Stern's account the only co-written piece they ever finished was a review of the movie *The Big Sleep* (CS 113).

In spring 1947 Justice and Jean Ross attended the Arts Forum Writers' Conference at the Women's College of the University of North Carolina, from which Jean had taken her bachelor's degree.[15] Ian Hamilton referred to this conference as "really a kind of Kenyon reunion" (125), as among the Kenyon graduates in attendance were Robert Lowell, Robie Macauley, John Thompson, Peter Taylor, and Randall Jarrell. A contingent of Kenyon students, including the brothers Anthony and Roger Hecht, drove to the conference from Gambier, Ohio. Besides Jean Ross and Donald Justice, the Chapel Hill group included Edgar Bowers, Paul Ramsey, and Richard Stern. "I remember our enormous interest and our feeling of partaking of the future," Jean wrote (CS 119). Poems by Justice, Bowers, and Ramsey appeared in the Arts Forum issue of *Coraddi*, the student literary magazine of the Women's College. As part of the conference, Robert Penn Warren discussed these poems. He said of some images in Justice's poems that they were "like Rube Goldberg contraptions." "Warren was quite right," Justice recalled, "and my feelings were only very slightly bruised. I couldn't say that any of the criticism was encouraging, except perhaps in the sense that the poems were taken seriously" (2001, 31–32).

In August 1947 Justice graduated from the University of North Carolina with a master's degree in English. He had written his thesis on the relationship between the poetry and prose of the Fugitive–Agrarians, "how the ideas you found in their prose criticism turned up in their poems as well, especially their hatred of the abstract" (Justice 2001, 29). The topic emphasizes the extent to which he was continuing his studies of the Southern literary tradition, for which he had previously considered himself a candidate. He later recalled that for "a brief period, three or four years perhaps," he considered himself a Southern writer. He was drawn by the "spell of Faulkner's wild and steamy prose" and the "innocent fairy-tale world Eudora Welty's early stories conjured up," but the South where he was born and grew up had little to do with what these authors wrote (PS 218–19).

On August 22 Donald Justice and Jean Ross were married. They moved to Miami, where Donald taught for a year at the University of Miami while Jean worked in the university library (CS 119). The newlyweds lived in his parents' garage apartment in northwest Miami.[16] Donald was busy teaching four sections of freshman composition and one of world literature (Justice 2001, 32). The following summer they spent a few weeks with Peter and Eleanor Ross Taylor in North Carolina. Justice later recalled an evening when his brother-in-law spoke of his writing "in such a way that it seemed to me that suddenly I saw what it was to *think* like a writer" (quoted in Alexander 104).

A year later Justice began graduate work at Stanford University. He had hoped to study with Yvor Winters, a copy of whose *In Defense of Reason*—a reprint of four books of critical prose—had been a wedding gift from Richard Stern. But Justice could only audit Winters's writing course, which the English Department chair deemed inappropriate for an entering graduate student (CS 120). Justice found the course a great pleasure even if Winters did not always like the poems that he handed in (ibid., 177). In the first class meeting, Winters read an excerpt from a poem by George Crabbe (1754–1832), a long passage of natural description in heroic couplets. The first assignment was to compose a similar passage in imitation of Crabbe's manner. Justice found the assignment rather easy to accomplish, a matter simply of repeating Crabbe's protocols of description. Having established the style of his imitation, the young poet wrote "Et Cetera" at the bottom of the page. The defender of reason was not amused.[17]

Because Jean's job at the geology library paid relatively little, Donald needed to keep his assistantship; in accordance with the department's practice, he taught two courses per term while taking only one. Frustrated with the enforced slow pace of Donald's progress, the couple decided to leave. The money that Donald won for placing second in a short story contest (for "The Doctor's Wife") bought their train ticket back to Miami, where once again Donald taught at the university and Jean worked at the library (CS 120–21; Justice 2001, 34). Even though his apprenticeship to Winters did not work out as he had hoped, Justice on several occasions paid tribute to Winters for teaching him the proper use of meter (PS 5; CS 178–79).

He taught at his undergraduate alma mater for two more years, during which his first book, *The Old Bachelor and Other Poems* (1951), was published by Pandanus Press, run by Preston Dettman, who worked at a Miami record store. Dettman owned a letterpress printer and published a handful of pamphlets such as Justice's *Old Bachelor* (CS 193–94), which consists of nine poems, several of which Justice "had written at Stanford with some hope of pleasing Winters" (Justice 2001, 35). According to the pamphlet's colophon, 240 copies were printed.

During this time in Miami, the Justices were part of a bohemian and artistic set centered in the Coconut Grove area. According to Jean's recollection, the Grove comprised several social strands—broadly speaking, the wealthy upper crust, the middle class, the rather poor, and the bohemians; the latter group was basically middle class, though its members tended to circulate with some freedom among the others. Having grown up on a farm (though with access to the books her brothers brought home from college), Jean found the world of the Grove fascinating and new.[18] Although Vaughn was a member of the bohemian set, he was often away. When he was in town, he helped his mother with a produce business (Justice 1998a, 65). Donald recalled him as someone who tended to get a job and keep it, at least while he stayed in one place.

Justice's poem "Portrait with One Eye" (CP 132) is about Vaughn, who wore a patch after losing an eye. The poem recounts:

> They robbed you of your ticket
> To the revolution, oh,
> And then they stomped you good.

The actual beating took place in Kansas City. When the police asked Vaughn his occupation, he responded "lyric poet." The poem also commemorates Vaughn's personal style:

> You who could scream across
>
> The square in Cuernavaca
> At a friend you hadn't seen
> For years, the one word, *bitch*,
> And turn away—that's style!

The person to whom Vaughn yelled across the square was another member of the Coconut Grove group, Gloria Grasmuck, who at one time worked as a translator under the Castro regime. She wrote a long poem about her experiences in Cuba and seemed offended when Justice recommended that she write the memoir in prose rather than verse. She was also a painter whose work Justice characterized as "conventional but good." Years later she worked in upstate New York for a priest with whom she eventually took up residence. Jean recalls Grasmuck with a Cheshire Cat smile, and a time that she and a friend came calling in funny clothes, like children playing dress-up. Donald remembered her hunched over a guitar, playing it slowly and sadly.[19]

Another member of the Grove was Eugene Rosenbloom, who was interested in writing and had ambitions to make comic films. He wrote a book with another denizen of the Grove, Don Martin, a cartoonist for *MAD* magazine. The book, much in the Martin style, is *Fester and Karbunkle on National Gorilla Suit Day*. When Rosenbloom and Justice were undergraduates at Miami, Justice directed a production of Rosenbloom's comic play *Beppo's Song*, in which the title character, to avoid the draft, pretends to be mentally unbalanced. Many years later Justice recalled a real-life sequel to the play. Unlike his character, Rosenbloom volunteered for military service; however, once enlisted, he found military life disagreeable, so he pretended to be mentally unbalanced. During his free time, he walked around picking up cigarette butts, and he made a habit of replying to officers, "Yes, mon capitaine." When he went to work as a college professor in California, he changed his name to Eugene Ralls, after the John Wayne character, the Byronic Captain Ralls, in *The Wake of the Red Witch* (1948).[20]

In late spring 1951, Justice was among the young professors let go by the University of Miami. Not sure what might come next, he and Jean stayed for a time with Peter and Eleanor Ross Taylor in Greensboro, North Carolina. Peter and his fellow Kenyon alumnus Robie Macauley suggested that Donald contact Paul Engle, who directed the Writers' Workshop at the State University of Iowa (later the University of Iowa), from which Macauley had recently graduated (Justice 2001, 35–36). Justice wrote to Engle and received in reply the "best teaching assistantship I could have possibly hoped for" (CS 180). He drove a cab in Miami to raise a stake for the move to Iowa City (ibid.).

As Stephen Wilbers explains, the workshop grew out of the university's, as well as Iowa City's, literary life (9–28). Under the guidance of Engle, who became the director in the 1940s, the workshop flourished. He had a genius for raising funds to finance the program and to provide fellowships for workshop students. Along with a fellowship, he gave Justice a winter suit made of heavy green tweed, for the young poet arrived from Miami unprepared for Iowa winters (Justice 1999, 29).

Engle's warm greeting and kindness were helpful antidotes to the Justices' underwhelming first impressions:

> We arrived on a bleak Saturday afternoon in late January of 1952, my wife Jean and I; arrived at the bus station downtown, for we had just completed an epic journey by cross-country bus from the winter sunshine of my hometown, Miami, Florida, to this midwestern wasteland—and, indeed, I remember that bleak and rather forbidding first impression the town made on us as the bus cruised past the first scattering of ugly midwestern houses, bits of lawn patchy with smudged snow, and on into the old-fashioned town center. We were very tired

and we knew no one. Paul Engle had put in a letter that we should phone him
upon arrival, and we did, a little doubtfully, expecting little. (Justice 1999, 27)

Engle drove the Justices to an apartment on Bowery Street, which he had
arranged for them to rent for sixty dollars a month. A week or so later, he
drove Donald in a snowstorm to a string quartet recital, and the elder poet's
handling of the car impressed the Floridian. Given the local culture, the
experience of the workshop, and the friends they made, Donald and Jean
eventually found the place to be "a Miranda's world—brave and new" (Justice 1999, 33).

Donald and Jean had a genius for collecting offbeat details and anecdotes throughout their life together. For instance, early in their time in Iowa
City, they ran into a man named Bill Couch, who had been a member of
the Snarks, the University of Miami literary society that Donald had be-
longed to. Couch was working as a window dresser for a department store
in downtown Iowa City; later, he was convicted of murdering his mother in
California. Another was the story, related to them by Robert Vaughn, of a
pool player named Johnnie Hadhad. The setting was Port Huron, Michigan,
where a pool game was taking place. At the conclusion of the game, when
it was clear that Hadhad was the loser, his dog ran into the street and the
path of an oncoming car in what appeared to be an act of suicide. I leave it to
the reader to decide whether this story belongs among the historical or the
apocryphal texts.

In May 1953, while Engle was out of town, Justice wrote him a letter that
reveals how much a part of the workshop's life the latter was already becoming. He mentions his collaboration with Engle on an O'Henry anthology
and recommends some people, notably Edgar Bowers and Richard Stern, for
projects and fellowships. He reports on the activities of writers in Iowa City:

> The Lowells [Robert Lowell and his wife] are happy here, and everybody is
> very happy to have them: a good piece of news, the plan to have them back
> regularly. Peter [Taylor] is well pleased with Kenyon, thinking of buying a
> house there (a Taylor vice). He thinks he will have the last story of a new book
> ready for fall publication—THE WIDOWS OF THORNTON. When he was here a
> couple of weeks back, he and Cal [Robert Lowell] made a big hit with a sort of
> Hope-Crosby act in the Shambaugh auditorium, Cal introducing him and Peter
> reading stories. We are planning to spend a few days in Gambier next month.[21]

He also mentions that he has poems forthcoming in the *New Yorker* and the
Hudson Review and that he and Jean are planning a month's vacation to visit
their parents in North Carolina and Florida.

While a student at the Writers' Workshop, Justice took courses from Paul
Engle, Karl Shapiro, Robert Lowell, and John Berryman. He paid tribute to
all four in his essay "A Miranda's World" but wrote most extensively of Berryman. Members of Berryman's class in the fall of 1954 were, besides Justice,
Jane Cooper, Henri Coulette, Robert Dana, William Dickey, Ronald (Rocco)
DiLorenzo, Shirley Eliason, Melvin Walker LaFollette, Philip Levine, Donald Petersen, Paul Petrie, and W. D. Snodgrass. As is well known, several
members of the group became prominent poets; others moved into a variety
of careers. DiLorenzo, for example, became an English professor specializing
in eighteenth-century British literature, Eliason a visual artist, LaFollette an
Episcopal priest.[22]

In writings about Berryman, two anecdotes about Justice regularly appear. One has to do with Justice's sonnet "The Wall." At the first meeting of
the course, Berryman discussed two sonnets, E. A. Robinson's "Many Are
Called" and John Manifold's "The Sirens." The first assignment was to produce a sonnet. Robert Dana showed me a copy of one of Berryman's notebook pages on which appear, under the heading "Assignment: a sonnet," the
following criteria: the Petrarchan form, with "strongly marked breaks"; one
"Elevated point"; and one "natural observation . . . or vivid image." The sonnet that Justice wrote in response to this assignment appears in *The Summer
Anniversaries* under the title "Sonnet" but appears in other collections as
"The Wall." It is a powerfully structured sonnet in the Petrarchan scheme,
where the turn—marked by the shift from the octave to the sestet—occurs
at Eve's eating of the forbidden fruit in the Garden of Eden. It includes such
natural observations (for Eden) as, "Angels were as common/As birds or
butterflies"; and it ends with the elevated moment, also a vivid image, of the
angels' "giant wings" unfurling (CP 13).

Although there is some variation among the accounts of the class session
in which this poem was discussed, all agree on Berryman's astonishment at
the sonnet's accomplishment. Some versions of the story that have circulated
orally say that Berryman saw the poem only at the beginning of class and
that his initial response to it occurred on the spot. Actually, Berryman had
seen the poem before class and had telephoned Justice the previous evening
to voice his appreciation.[23] At the beginning of the class session, as Rocco
DiLorenzo reports, Berryman asked Henri Coulette to lead off the discussion
of the sonnet. Coulette said, "It makes a nice impression," to which Berryman replied, "It makes a *very* nice impression." Berryman then led a discussion of the poem for much of the two-hour session.[24]

The second anecdote illustrates what a difficult friend and mentor Berryman could be. Around three or four one morning, he telephoned Justice and told him that he was thinking of committing suicide. Justice went to his apartment, which he and Jean had previously rented, and found Berryman "sitting on the floor . . . regarding an open case of old-fashioned razors." Justice's account continues: "The sight was too much for me. I felt faint and had to lie down on the sofa. He became immediately all concern and consideration, hurrying down the hall to the bathroom to fetch damp cloths with which to chafe my wrists and so on" (Justice quoted in Haffenden 240). Around dawn the two went into town for breakfast and then repaired to the Justices' apartment, where Berryman slept in an easy chair until the afternoon (see Mariani 279).

Justice graduated from Iowa in 1954 with a doctorate in English. His dissertation, titled "Beyond the Hunting Woods and Other Poems," consists of twenty-two poems, some of which would appear in his published books. Many had already appeared in *Furioso, Hudson Review, Ladies Journal* (London), *Mademoiselle,* the *New Yorker,* and *Poetry.* Concerning Justice's oral examination, Marvin Bell remembered: "One day, the poet James Crenner, nervous about his Ph.D. oral, asked me to sit in the room where he could see me. Jim was a terrific academic student, among other things. When the questioning ended, I made a move to leave but was told I should stay. The committee then spoke of how good Jim's oral had been and one added, 'I've heard only one better oral in all the years, and that was Donald Justice's.'"[25] Thus was the brilliant note on which Justice's formal education came to a close.

After Donald's graduation, he and Jean traveled to Europe on a Rockefeller Foundation grant (Wilbers 102). An undated postcard that Donald wrote to Paul Engle reports: "capitals of Europe too expensive for Rockefeller budget." They therefore planned to return to the States and stay in Miami. Justice had managed to make some progress in writing and publication, with poems in the November issue of *Poetry* and the fall issue of *Accent* and "2 good-sized poems done & a story underway." News had reached them concerning Berryman in Iowa City: "We were a good deal upset to hear about the Berryman business, though no report we've had has quite made clear what happened; I do hope sincerely that everything has worked out smoothly after that & that the Workshop is flourishing as usual, that there are some good new students etc." No doubt, the "Berryman business" was the poet's arrest after a late-night drunken altercation with his landlord. Berryman had returned to Iowa City to teach at the workshop, but after this incident and his appearance before the university deans, he was dismissed (see Haffenden 242–44).

By December 4, 1954, the Justices' difficulties extended beyond budgetary concerns, as he wrote in a letter:

> Don Petersen or Mike may have mentioned how unhappy Jean and I have been abroad and, anyhow, I couldn't bring myself to repeat such an ordinary little tale of woe. I've written only the two poems here, for one thing; on the other hand, they're about as good as I could have reasonably hoped for (I used to hope for miracles, of course). There may even have been, without my knowledge, some recharging of the spirit or whatever, but I'm inclined to doubt it. As for the future, we reason that we'll be happier and can work better in familiar surroundings; that means, for the duration of the fellowship, trying Miami, where my family and some of our old friends are.

Justice sounds some characteristic notes here concerning the shrinking of formerly grand hopes and of making due in diminished circumstances. If, among the cracked sidewalks, all is forlorn save for the golden names, one has at least the realm of language—the place of the name—in which to work.

After the Rockefeller fellowship, Justice took a teaching position at the University of Missouri at Columbia, where he encountered some unexpected success: "I'm becoming reconciled to teaching and even, by all evidences, a popular teacher, something I certainly never expected to be."[26] Life as a professor of literature provided Justice with a further way of integrating life and art, a way of making a living with literature.

The job at Missouri "might have extended itself indefinitely,"[27] but he took a job at Hamline University, in St. Paul, Minnesota, beginning in fall 1956.

In fall 1957 he returned to Iowa City as a lecturer, thus beginning his long association with the Writers' Workshop as a teacher. His relief at receiving the job is evident in a letter to Engle: "And thanks not only for the job, which seems a godsend (the way I felt about Hamline), but for the doubled check as well."[28] Donald and Jean spent July and August 1957 in Miami and then moved to Iowa City. By the end of the decade, Justice would be teaching at the workshop with Paul Engle, Vance Bourjaily, and Ray B. West (Wilbers 96).

Through these years of teaching and travel, Justice remained in touch with Robert Vaughn. In a January 1958 letter from Puerto Rico, Vaughn sounded some rather downtrodden notes in his observations of New York: "In New York there was almost no one left, Stanley on the coast, others dead or in jail; although I did see Jack Spencer reading an Arabic newspaper in the

Kettle of Fish and Franz Kline painting those big black lines on white canvas. And Miles who is selling pretty well." Then on May 30 of the same year, Vaughn wrote from the Virgin Islands, on letterhead that reads "St. C The St. Croix by the Sea": "I'm now asst. mgr. at this hotel, trying to save loot for one more trip. You'll have to forgive me if I sound rather illiterate but you can imagine what these jobs do to the dream." I take "the dream" to refer to the dedication to art, especially poetry, that Justice and Vaughn shared.

In a letter postmarked July 17, 1958, Vaughn wonders about the possibility of coming to Iowa for a master's degree. The letter begins, "I'm preparing for an Anegada trip and wishing I could get to Cuba and writing a little." The mention of Anegada is noteworthy, for it shows up in one of Justice's Vaughn poems, titled "Hell" (CP 214), which is spoken by Vaughn. Justice's note to the poem indicates that parts of the few lines following this poem's line six (which itself is quoted from a poem of Vaughn's titled "The Spell") "are freely adapted from another poem of his, 'The Black Rose'" (CP 281). The letter of Vaughn's from the Virgin Islands includes a typescript of "The Black Rose," which begins

> When I was very young I thought that love
> Would sieze [sic] her creature like a great white bird
> And take him south to see stone roses, talk
> With Gordon Pym among the ashes settling there.
> But that's before I learned the war of wills, the care
> And resolution of the ambiguities that stalk
> My every line and merge leech-like upon the word.

In his essay "Oblivion: Variations on a Theme," Justice says of Vaughn's work that "there are fragments and stanzas possessing, if you have a taste for it, great beauty of a certain high romantic kind" (1998a, 66). Certainly, "beauty of a certain high romantic kind" is what Vaughn was after.

Among the ways that Justice identifies Vaughn in this essay is as a revolutionary, and indeed there is much talk of Cuba and Castro in Vaughn's letters. His poem "Another Lent," with the subscript "on Ernesto Guevara," includes the lines

> Che sees
> The Manifest of Friedrich Engels hang
> Above the snow and fog of London
> Singing the song like a Lutheran nun.[29]

In a letter written from Havana, Vaughn makes the following pronounce-
ments:

> Dear Don,
>
> Many things, muchas cosas, and the rose unfolds. If you were here you would
> have written a bunch of stories and a lot of poems. I got in three in three
> weeks.
>
> Fidel and Che are making what we once called history. It sings in the air
> like those wires that Leon Rapollo once thought he heard or heard.[30]

For Vaughn the life of writing and the life of politics often went together,
and both were of a certain "high romantic kind." But the devotion to writing
remained primary, and sometimes the politics got in the way. In a letter from
Key West, he speaks of going to Cuba four times in six weeks, and then he
comments, "But there's too much action there in Habana to think or write
very much." By way of contrast, he describes Key West as "a grey and sometimes windy, quiet town, where one can work." The letter ends with several
admonitions relating to the artistic vocation: "Keep writing, write to me, and
hear the new Thelonious records if you get a chance."[31]

■ S O L E M N
V O W S

Justice's first full-length volume, *The Summer Anniversaries*, won the Lamont Poetry Award for 1959 and appeared from Wesleyan University Press in 1960. The reviews were somewhat mixed but on the whole favorable. One criticism, which echoed variously through Justice's career, was that the poems were too "literary." In other words, some critics complained that the poems' influences showed too conspicuously, and some that the poems took other literary texts as their subject matter or point of departure. But Justice's work resists a binary opposition between art and life. Even in the case of an artist aspiring to live for art alone—as Justice discusses in his 1946 letter to Barbara Pearson quoted in the previous chapter—the opposition cannot be maintained. As I recall him saying on at least one occasion, literature was an important part of his life, so one could well expect a concern with it to show up in his writing. While literature could never be the whole of his life, it was nevertheless an important part of his life experience.

But some reviewers did not see the literature and the life as yet sufficiently integrated. David Galler, for example, maintained, "Justice is at the mercy of his masters" (CS 212). Howard Nemerov's notice of Justice's literariness was more positive in its assessment: "Although his manner is not yet fully disengaged from that of certain modern masters, whom he occasionally echoes, his own way of doing things does in general come through" (ibid., 209). George P. Elliott extended Nemerov's view in his observation that the emerging style of the book negotiates in complex terms influences of strong poets of the past, along with the demands of Justice's own taste. Further, Elliott observes that although much of the book sounds like Justice's accomplished contemporaries—one might think, for example, of Nemerov (who had published four volumes of poetry before 1960), Richard Wilbur (three volumes), Anthony Hecht (whose *A Summoning of Stones* had appeared in 1954), and James Merrill (whose first two mature collections had appeared)—one can also pick up the distinctive voice. Elliott thus responds to those reviewers who found *The Summer Anniversaries* to be derivative and too preoccupied with matters of craft: "His reach rarely exceeds his grasp. But he aspires to more than carpentry too. He is formal to the point of elegance, and for poetic elegance nothing but respect is in order" (CS 215). But then this son of a carpenter surely had respect for the elegance of which good carpentry is capable.

As to Justice's elegance, it is helpful to recall that the word comes from the Latin *eligere*, meaning to select. Poetic elegance consists to no small degree in the judicious and proper selection of words, or as Richard Howard put it in his 1971 discussion of Justice's poems, "a consistent choice of words and their arrangement in the exemplification of a single taste" (CS 53). This single taste has more to do with Justice's consistently high standards than with, say, a single style, for one of Justice's great strengths was his constant experimentation with various styles, as well as with a variety of approaches to the making of poems. At the service of his high standards, he incorporated into his work an array of cultural materials—including the literatures of several languages, arts other than literature, and philosophical and theological themes, not to mention his own life experience.

But even with this great variety, certain emphases and themes emerge. For example, many of the poems explore entry into and negotiation of the everyday world. Taken on a grander scale, this theme includes negotiation of the world of history, as opposed to the realm of the gods or of an Edenic space before history began. At the same time, this realm outside of history is recalled under an erasure that recognizes it never really was. The resulting ironic vision—the recollection of a realm that did not exist—provides one of the ways that Justice found to write in a postmodern mode of the sublime. I discuss this mode in greater detail below; for now, suffice it to say that Justice's poems achieve the sublime—a vision of the larger than life and potentially threatening, viewed from an aesthetic distance—by adverting to its unavailability. In other words, Justice achieves the sublime by alluding to the old conceptions that he erases. His sublime is the moment of sublime loss.

The poem in *The Summer Anniversaries* that most conspicuously confronts such a moment is the "Sonnet," later retitled "The Wall" (CP 13), which he wrote for Berryman's course. In his review of the book, Nemerov quite insightfully sees this poem as central to the whole volume: "The chief subject of Mr. Justice's poems is the journey from innocence to experience, the Fall, domestically reflected most often in reminiscences of childhood, that strange, lost land about which there is nevertheless 'something familiar.' The first seven poems, for instance, vary this subject, while the eighth makes explicit what has been happening by being about the expulsion from Eden" (CS 209). As several have pointed out (see, for example, Jarman 2002), "The

Wall" condenses into the "little song" of the sonnet form the story of Milton's *Paradise Lost*; for example, Milton's great epic is the only source, as far as I know, for Eve's dream, which Justice invokes. Justice focuses Milton's grand epic of the Fall into one fourteen-line poem.

Although this sonnet covers the Adam and Eve story through the exit from the Garden, it aptly focuses its most dramatic moment on the "expulsion from Eden," meaning the transition "from innocence to experience," the entry into history. As Samuel Johnson pointed out, one "inconvenience" of Milton's epic is that it "comprises neither human actions nor human manners. The man and woman who act and suffer are in a state which no other man or woman can ever know" (1861, 181). We must therefore read Milton's poem in a state of radical alienation. It is only after Adam and Eve take "their solitary way" at the end of the poem that they become legible to human understanding in time as we know it. Justice's sonnet calls attention precisely to this transition. Significantly for Justice's work, however, this moment of alienation from the place of original unity is also the moment when the sublime occurs. As the "giant wings" unfurl, the angels are transformed from creatures "as common / As birds or butterflies," but which look "more human," into the awe-inspiring, potentially terrifying beings now guarding the closed gates of Eden. It may be that in Justice's version of the story, Adam and Eve were in some sense existing in the midst of the sublime all along, but they do not know it or experience until it is lost. Indeed, "As long as the wings were furled, they felt no awe"; awe, a necessary component of the experience of the sublime, escapes them until they have prompted those mighty creatures to unfurl their wings. They can only catch a glimpse of the sublime in the precise moment of its loss.

Another term for the act of looking back to a lost Eden is nostalgia, the "longing for a past that has never quite existed, with its concomitant of feelings of loss and displacement" (Perloff 20), which has been the ruin of many a promising writer. But Justice turned this potential weakness into an uncanny strength. He has long been known as a poet of complicated nostalgias. As William Logan points out in "The Midnight of Nostalgia," Justice's nostalgias work primarily as "antisentiment" (CS 88); that is, they investigate the experiences of longing, loss, and displacement rather than indulging in them. Logan's essay focuses on the span of Justice's poems from the new pieces appearing in *Selected Poems* (1979) through the poems of *The Sunset Maker* (1987), but I believe that with the *Collected Poems* (2004) now before us, we can discern the development of this complex and critical vision throughout the poet's career. Even in the early poems of *The Summer*

Anniversaries, one can witness the workings of such a reflective nostalgia as Logan identifies not as an "emotional consolation of submission," but rather as something more like the "religious desolation of confession" (CS 88). If much of the poetic efforts of Justice's era, as of others, indulged in nostalgia with the abandon of Father Tetzel's sale of indulgences, then Justice's poems may be taken as so many theses calling for reform.

The term *nostalgia* was coined in the seventeenth century by the Swiss doctor Johannes Hofer, with reference to a condition that afflicted such displaced persons as domestic help serving in Germany and France and "Swiss soldiers fighting abroad" (Boym 3). The coinage comes from Greek roots meaning a longing to return home. This form of homesickness, though, has come to be more strongly associated with the idealization of the past and a refusal of the complications of history. In *The Future of Nostalgia* (2001) Svetlana Boym posits a sense of the condition peculiar to the modern age, characterized by a "mourning for the impossibility of mythical return" to a "home that is both physical and spiritual, the edenic unity of time and space before entry into history" (8). If I am correct in extending Logan's observations about Justice's nostalgias back to *The Summer Anniversaries* and extending Nemerov's observations about "The Wall" beyond the confines of the first volume, as well as in reading this sonnet as an important key to all of Justice's work, then we might see in the whole trajectory of poems a self-aware version of this longing for a place of unity before history began.

Justice's poems are nothing if not self-aware. Boym distinguishes broadly between two kinds of nostalgia, each specializing in a different understanding, or mode of awareness, of the longing to return home. As she points out (41), these are not absolute types, but rather discernible tendencies whose manifestations may include characteristics of the other type. One tendency emphasizes the idealized sense of home, and the other emphasizes the experiences of longing and loss. The former tendency, which Boym calls *restorative nostalgia*, denies that it is nostalgia at all, for it takes itself too seriously as a longing and search for literal truth as it seeks to rebuild the lost home. The latter tendency, *reflective nostalgia*, "dwells in *algia*, in longing and loss, the imperfect process of remembrance" (41). This kind of nostalgia remains aware of its own idealizations; it is "more concerned with historical and individual time, with the irrevocability of the past and human finitude" (49). I recall Justice on one occasion talking about his enjoyment of taking back roads on driving trips because he experienced a certain nostalgia in doing so, and because he enjoyed such feelings. This self-awareness of reflective nostalgia is also the consciousness one encounters in the poems.

I take Nemerov's cue that the "first seven poems" of *The Summer An-niversaries* vary the subject of the "journey from innocence to experience," while the "eighth ["The Wall"] makes explicit what has been happening by being about the expulsion from Eden." Therefore, I consider each of the opening seven poems in turn before returning to "The Wall." "Anniversaries" (CP 5–6) begins with the line "Great Leo roared at my birth," which playfully, even parodically, announces the poet's entry into a strikingly unified world, one that functions as a total and totalizing system. The poem's opening section shows evidence of what Timothy J. Reiss calls "patterning discourse," which assumes the radical unity of knower, sign, and known in a homogenous system according to which everything—from animal forms to the names of stars—carries significance about the world (40–114). In the poem's rather cartoonish version of a unified world, in which not only do the stars announce the birth, but also the earth shakes and relatives arrive to prophesy the career to come, all is focused on the newborn child. Here the poem speaks from the child's narcissistic point of view that it also gently satirizes. All the more striking, then, is the sense of alienation in the second section as the child, now ten years old, awakens where the goldenrod and broom are merely plants blooming in vacant lots, rather than representations or harbingers of some larger meaning. As he is "wheeled superb in a chair," he is still well taken care of, but now he experiences "Standing a little off"—something of the alienation that will develop into the adult artist's depersonalized stance.

In the poem's third section, the speaker moves more explicitly toward his artistic vocation. Now seventeen, he is thinking quite seriously about literature, having guessed

> That the "really great loneliness"
> Of James's governess
> Might account for the ghost
> On the other side of the lake.

He has been reading *The Turn of the Screw* by Henry James (see especially page 14); the lines about the effects of "great loneliness" not only reflect on the young man's relative solitude, but also anticipate the ghostly presences that will enter Justice's poems (see, for example, "The Grandfathers" and "Invitation to a Ghost"). For now the young man spends his after-school hours at the piano, fingering the "ripe heart" of Chopin while "boys outside in the dirt" kick, "up and down, their ball."

By the age of thirty, in the poem's final section, the speaker comes into a full realization of his loss and alienation. Like the couple exiting Eden in "The Wall," the speaker of "Anniversaries" catches a glimpse of something grand at this moment of realizing its loss, a "momentary flash" as the sunset briefly lights up the trees "like/The candles upon a cake." This passing congruence between the birthday candles and the flash of sunlight in the trees suggests something of the grand unity both fantasized and parodied in the opening section; but it is only a hint, a remnant or fragment, of such a worldview, no sooner glimpsed than gone. As the speaker informs us,

Yet there was time to wish
Before the light could die,
If I had known what to wish,
As once I must have known.

If ever he knew what to wish for, the knowledge is gone, as is the moment of the wish, along with the flash in the trees and the fantasy of such wholeness and unity as would allow mere wishes to come to be.

As Walter Ong (1982, 103–8) has pointed out, alienation can be a very good thing, for knowledge requires both proximity and distance. To know the world and ourselves, we must experience some degree of alienation. Growth in knowledge and artistic accomplishment often means violating an earlier and comforting sense of oneself and the world. If the radical unity with which "Anniversaries" opens were in fact the case, nothing new or unpredictable could occur, for all meanings would already be established—the world to come, like the newborn's career, already known. Were this the structure of the cosmos, and were the "brilliant career" prophesied in the poem one of artistic pursuit, then the poet would be born into a world that scarcely needed him. An artistic vocation is much more meaningful and urgent in an ambiguous and open-ended cosmos, one in which new meanings are still to come. It is a vision of history as open-ended that gives force to the axiom invoked by Ezra Pound: "Artists are the antennae of the race" (1934, 610). Fully alienated from the unified sense of the world that opens the poem, the speaker is prepared to take up his artistic vocation.

The following poem, "Song" (CP 7), returns again to a vision of unity in a language edging toward archaism, a hint of nostalgia for an older language style associated with an older mode of perception:

Morning opened
Like a rose,

And the snow on the roof
Rose-color took.

Because Dante is among the strong undercurrents of Justice's poems, it is
difficult not to hear a remote allusion in these opening lines to the vision
of heavenly unity at the beginning of the thirty-first canto of the *Paradiso*:
"Then in the shape of a white rose / Was shown to me the sacred legion."[1] By
the fourth line of Justice's "Song," however, the "rose" comes to function as
a marker of color rather than a unifying shape, and the poem's light not only
fails but also falls as this moment of rose-colored radiance fades:

And the lamps went out.
Brightness fell down
From the steeple clock
To the rows of shops . . .

Dwelling up with the steeple, this light may remind the reader of ways that
light has functioned for centuries as a symbol of transcendence (see Blumenberg), though falling from the clock, it here brings a reminder of time
into the everyday world. If I may attribute to Justice a moment of punning,
the tenuously transcendent *rose* at the poem's start has now become the
rows of shops of this everyday world in time. Nevertheless, this "Song" commemorates a world with a fairy-tale sheen, though the tone remains impersonal and remote. For one thing, the poem's touches of archaism (such as
the inversions of word order) serve to keep the poem's world at a distance.
For another,

. . . all that day
Was a fairy tale
Told once in a while
To a good child.

The third-person stance of this final line swerves away from what had
seemed a personal reminiscence of this particular day. The presence of the
"good child" to whom the fairy tale is told distances the poem and its sense
of the world even further—the description of this "fairy tale" day is not addressed to the reader, but rather to this figure in the poem.

   The two poems that follow, "To a Ten-Months Child" (CP 8) and "The
Poet at Seven" (CP 9), continue the meditation on childhood and the fall
into history. The first directly addresses a newborn child—the "M. M." of the
dedication is Megan Merker, the elder daughter of the printer Kim Merker,

a friend of the Justices in Iowa City[2]—in terms of her departure from the
unified world of the womb. "So recently displaced," the child now exists in a
world of multiplicity

> among
>
> So many strangers, all
> Babbling a strange tongue.

Like the fall into a multiplicity of tongues in the Tower of Babel episode of
the Bible (Genesis 11:1–9), this fall into language occasions a more complex
vision of the world. It is this "strange tongue," the language that constitutes
the primary material to be shaped by the poet, that is the instrument of multiplicity and the separation from the unified world that it recalls.

As its title indicates, "The Poet at Seven" takes the young poet as its subject matter. Walter Martin (CS 48) has pointed out that this poem echoes
Rimbaud's "Les Poètes de sept an." Ironically, in Justice's poem, in playing at
animal life, constructing a lean-to so that he can "on all fours crawl in it like
a bear/To lick his wounds in secret, in his lair," the young poet would escape the language without which the poem could not come to be. The poem
gives voice to an impulse to reverse the journey from such a "lately crossed"
ocean as the previous poem recounts, and to crawl into the womblike space
of the lair, protected from the world's weather. The poem thus registers an
association of the nostalgic impulse with the impulse to return to the womb.
In fantasizing a life without human language, the poem calls attention to
language as the sign, the constant play of differentiation that both signals
and creates, articulates and enforces separation from an originating sense of
wholeness. This separation is the cleavage, the breaking away necessary for
growth to occur (see Ong 1977, 17–49). Language itself becomes the sign of
woundedness that enables humans to know and talk about ourselves and
the world. "The Poet at Seven" recounts a momentary attempt to turn away
from this necessary and enabling experience of woundedness and fragmentation. All of the forms of play that the poem recounts—flying a paper air-
plane, whirling around and falling, squatting in a vacant lot—occur as games
without words. Similarly wordless is the concluding interaction in which
"someone dear" comes to get the child and "whip him down the street, but
gently, home." The child returns home but not to the womb; rather, home
is here where other people live, meaning that home in this poem is a place
of human interaction and language. Returning to the realm of language, he
returns to the realm of the wounded human consciousness, a woundedness
signaled by the subdued violence of the gentle, homeward whipping.

"The Snowfall" (CP 10) presents us with "Fragments of a pathetic culture." Although the precise "culture" represented here is not specified, the details listed provide enough clues—"lost mittens of children" and a "single, bright, detasseled snow cap"—to guess that it is the culture of childhood. Actually, the opening description of "footprints leading nowhere" in the snow suggests that the speaker is describing a yard where children have been playing, but the scene then becomes a representation of the entire culture of childhood as the kind of "doomed" republic one encounters at the opening of the poem "Childhood." By defamiliarizing the scene—first by comparing it to the "classic landscapes of dreams" and then by referring to it as the remnants of a "culture" (rather than as a yard), as well as by withholding the precise object of description—Justice allows the suggestion that this speaker is engaged in a kind of ethnographic investigation, trying to figure out what kinds of fragments he is looking at. They have captured his imagination, for there "is something familiar about this country." This line is the one that Nemerov quoted: "childhood, that strange, lost land about which there is nevertheless 'something familiar.'" The poem is a vague recollection of innocence from the point of view of experience, and while the recollections are slow to emerge, by the end of the poem the speaker comes to realize that what he is gazing at are in effect the fragments of his own childhood world, now gone:

> Slowly now we begin to recall
>
> The terrible whispers of our elders
> Falling softly about our ears
> In childhood, never believed till now.

One of the elders himself now, he addresses (most immediately) his fellow elders who have also forgotten the world of innocence that is in fragments.

Even though "The Snowfall" is not cast as a dream, the reference in its opening line to "The classic landscapes of dreams" casts the whole poem in a twilight reminiscent of dreams; the idea of dreaming, with its ambiguous and shifting scenes and sensations, becomes a mediating structure for the experience recounted in the poem. There is seldom if ever in Justice's poems any pretence of facing the world head on, if "head on" is taken to mean without mediation. For these poems disclose again and again that human knowledge of the world is always mediated by structures that make understanding possible: language, art, interpretive frameworks, memories, dreams. Rather than trying to circumvent such mediation for the sake of getting at some supposedly primal experience, the poems engage fully with these mediating structures—sometimes even making them primary points of focus—so that the experiences they mediate, recount, and create can be all the richer, all the more real for the inclusion of what makes them possible. The idea of some kind of primal experience, whether of the garden or the womb, is always a back formation based on experiences that one has had subsequent to the idealized primal moment. Having experience means having always already fallen into the world of time, history, fragmentation. We experience the primal moment as always and only lost. In "The Snowfall," the world that is lost is by all evidence a "pathetic culture," that is, a culture evoking pathos, a culture finally inadequate, as all cultures in some sense prove to be. One reason that a culture's traditions must remain on the move is that culture can never be a final achievement. There is always one kind of "frantic migration" or another going on as human experience keeps pushing culture and tradition to move on, to change in response to changing conditions and questions, urgencies, and needs. It would seem that the "terrible whispers" of the elders in "The Snowfall" were warning the child that this world would not last. Even the elders, the voices of tradition, warn that tradition must stay in motion.

"Landscape with Little Figures" (CP 11) continues the series of journeys from innocence to experience by beginning with a world of rather generic details: "There were some pines, a canal, a piece of sky." Although these are details of a world, they hang in relative abstraction, for there is no narrative or description creating relationships among them. As soon as the details move into a narrative, the world disclosed becomes complex:

> The pines are the houses now of the very poor,
> Huddled together, in a blue, ragged wind.

Not only is this place of "ragged wind" inhabited by "the very poor"—people whose experience is most conspicuously caught up in day-to-day struggles—the canal is now "mud flats," and there is a "red ball lost in the weeds." Although the red ball might be a relatively minor loss, its color remotely calls up the fruit, the apple, of *Paradise Lost*, the eating of which occasions the loss of Eden and the fragmentation of the world into history. As this opening series of poems in *The Summer Anniversaries* recounts various versions of the Fall, so Milton often hovers nearby. (Milton and Dante are Justice's two great precursors of more remote ages, as Baudelaire, Wallace Stevens, and Eliot are his great proximate precursors; on the influence of Stevens and Eliot, see Hudgins 656–59.) After the mention of the red ball in the weeds, the poem takes on a character of loss, belatedness, and valediction: "It's winter, it's after supper, it's goodbye." Finally, the speaker must bid farewell to this picture of the ragged world: "O goodbye to the houses, the children, the little red ball." He even says goodbye to the "pieces of sky that will go on now falling for days." This whole world picture is in fragments and will go on fragmenting "for days," even after the poem is over.

The poem that immediately precedes "The Wall"—"On the Death of Friends in Childhood" (CP 12)—is a brief meditation that, of these opening seven poems, most conspicuously exits the everyday world, preparing the way for the mythic story of Adam and Eve. As the title indicates, this poem—which I think remains in the most select of Justice's finest[3]—concerns those who, because they have died young, never make it out of the "lost land" of childhood. As "Anniversaries" opens with a cartoonish version of a unified world that the poem exits, so "On the Death of Friends in Childhood" opens with cartoonish versions of the hereafter, those "bearded in heaven" and the "bald of hell" (like the old representations of the bearded patriarchs in heaven and of devils with their shiny red pates), which the poem eschews. The poem swerves away from any traditional notion of a life hereafter, for if there is "anywhere" that "We" shall meet the dead, it is "in the deserted schoolyard at twilight." We find ourselves once more in a twilit and dreamlike world of memory.

The great poem looming behind this one is Emily Dickinson's "Because I could not stop for Death." The fourth and fifth lines of Justice's poem, recalling the dead friends of childhood "Forming a ring, perhaps, or joining hands / In games whose very names we have forgotten," echo a moment of Dickinson's famous ride with Death: "We passed the School, where Children strove / At Recess—in the Ring." This ring of the childhood game, suggestive of the closure and continuity of Edenic fantasy, is what the speakers of both poems have left behind. In Justice's vision, the hereafter that exists is the one that memory provides. The command or request at the end of "On the Death of Friends in Childhood"—"Come, memory, let us seek them there in the shadows"—implies an expectation that the speaker and memory personified will encounter moments of further recollection. The poem continues to be haunted by these past lives as the speaker searches the shadows.

Part of what remains unclear about this poem is the identity of who is included in the pronoun "We" in the opening line. Might this be the speaker and memory? Perhaps the speaker and others of his generation who survived childhood? Maybe the speaker addresses some collective sense of memory. Or is the speaker addressing his personal memory in the context of collective memory? Given the fairly generic imagery of the poem, along with the almost archetypal Dickinson poem that stands behind it, I take the latter to be a strong possibility—that the memory traversed through much of the poem, and addressed at the end, is in fact a collective memory, without which personal memory has no context in which to function. The imagery of the playground works quite fittingly with the place of collective memory, which Boym points out "can be seen as a playground, not a graveyard of multiple individual recollections" (54). This is a vision of collective memory as thoroughly located within a culture, rather than separated off into a transcendent realm. The closing line thus works as an invocation to personal memory to walk the playground of collective memory in a mood and mode of recollection. There are no immortal shades in the poem. These "shadows" of memory, both collective and personal, are all that exist of those who have died. It is part of the function of art to make these memories memorable. As Justice put it in his essay "Meters and Memory," one "motive for much if not all art" is "to keep memorable what deserves to be remembered" (PS 170). The poem takes on a quasi-ritual function that in effect says, as in the closing line of Justice's "Sonnet to My Father," "Yet while I live, you do not wholly die" (CP 23).

"On the Death of Friends in Childhood" leads to Justice's version of a mythic journey from innocence to experience. As Milton's great epic provides a version of the Fortunate Fall—the traditional paradox that even though the original sin was a real transgression, it becomes through the action of the divine in history the occasion of greater recompense, the salvific work of the Messiah—so Justice's "The Wall" (CP 13) recounts a fortunate fall into knowledge, not so much knowledge of good and evil (as in the biblical and Miltonic versions), as knowledge of the world. As the opening lines emphasize, Adam and Eve in the Garden do not realize that the "world" of their experience is circumscribed by the wall enclosing them. Not only do they not yet know what the wall might be closing in or closing out, they do not even realize that it exists. What they know are the animals of their immediate world, along with the creatures that most resemble human beings, the angels, which look "more human" than birds or butterflies. Seeing the angels while their "wings were furled," Adam and Eve experience them only as more of the same; even these most sublime, or potentially sublime, of creatures do not yet appear sublime. All is commonplace.

But as in *Paradise Lost*, the first couple in "The Wall" is also in some sense already beyond the confines of this enclosed world even before the act of transgression. J. Hillis Miller attributes such complexity as this to the "luxuriance of Milton's poetic power" (1991, 294), and we might attribute something very like such power to Justice's work as well. In Milton's poem, even though Adam and Eve have not yet eaten the fruit of the tree of knowledge of good and evil, they nevertheless possess some rudimentary knowledge of evil, and to the extent that they possess this knowledge, they have already left the confines of their world of original unity. For example, in Book Five after Adam hears Eve's account of her dream, which neither of them knows was inspired by Satan, Adam responds,

> nor can I like
> This uncouth dream, of evil sprung I fear;
> Yet evil whence? in thee can harbour none,
> Created pure. (lines 97–100)

Adam himself is perplexed to find that evil and its knowledge have already infiltrated the Garden.

In a similar way, the couple in Justice's poem find themselves already beyond the confines of their world:

> They could find no flaw
> In all of Eden: this was the first omen.

The first omen of the transgression to come is not that there is no flaw; rather, it is that they were looking for a flaw to begin with. By merely looking, they are already beginning to conceive, however vaguely, of a framework other than the present state of affairs—one that would show a flaw in this world. Further, looking for a flaw implies at least the beginnings of some dissatisfaction with this present world. This stirring to think beyond the confines of their enclosed and seemingly perfect world is the first tear in the seamless fabric of the Garden's perfection. Their seeking for a flaw becomes the very flaw that they seek, a sign of dissatisfaction with a world that they do not yet know is enclosed.

This moment of their seeking—which seems almost instinctual, an action of a pre-reflective, pre-moral kind—is the beginning of their movement outside the Garden. This seeking works as a moment of what Joseph Donceel (55–63) styles the dynamism of the human intellect, the mind always finding itself already beyond whatever intellectual enclosure it happens to be in. Even thinking of one's cognitive framework as a framework implies that one is already in some sense beyond it, for the idea of a framework stands as one possibility where others might function to disclose other areas of actuality. A framework that is uncritically accepted is not seen as a framework—as "restorative nostalgia" denies that it is nostalgia—but rather simply as the way things are. Seeing a framework as one's set of assumptions and convictions already means seeing it critically, which is not the same as seeing it as necessarily false, but rather as limited, as one valid though not comprehensive or exhaustive version of the story. Conceiving of a framework as thus limited implies a movement already outside or beyond it, the primal dynamism that constitutes the basic condition for further investigation.

By the time of the sestet, after the fruit has already been eaten, the coming into knowledge is a foregone conclusion. As in Milton, the physical eating of the fruit is anticlimactic. In Milton's version Eve's eating of the fruit occupies the space of two feet, "she pluck'd, she eat" (bk. 9, line 781), and Adam's, three metrical feet of rather pointed understatement: "he scrupl'd not to eat" (ibid., line 997). Justice elides the physical eating almost entirely—"As for the fruit, it had no taste at all"—alluding to the act only to emphasize, in the tastelessness, that physically the act hardly registers; the real weight is in its implication, which is profound. The lines that follow Justice's version of eating the fruit emphasize that actually the couple has in some sense known about the wall and the world beyond it all along, or at least they have been repeatedly told about these things:

> They had been warned of what was bound to happen.
> They had been told of something called the world.
> They had been told and told about the wall.
> They saw it now; the gate was standing open.

This implicit or inchoate knowledge is in the process of becoming explicit and thematic. The parallelism of these lines emphasizes that they are coming into more explicit awareness: they had been warned, they had been told, they saw it now.

But the most startling and disruptive vision that arises from this emerging state of knowledge is that of the angels, who no longer have the human look that they had earlier in the poem: "As they advanced, the giant wings unfurled." Given the earlier line "As long as the wings were furled, they felt no awe," the implication of this closing line is that here Adam and Eve, at the moment of losing Eden, feel awe for the first time. Not only do they now have a vision of the world outside the wall, their vision of the world that they have lost is transformed, for here it takes on an awe-inspiring grandeur. For the first time, they have a vision of the sublime, of something larger than life and awe-inspiring, potentially terrifying, beyond the charms and beauties of the world they have known thus far. But they can have this vision of Eden only as they are losing it; the great wings unfurl in response to their eating of the fruit. The moment of the sublime is the moment of sublime loss. It is the kind of moment that recurs in Justice's poems, one that colors the vision of history outside the wall; history is where the sublime no longer occurs but is only recalled.

Justice's work, "The Wall" in particular, resonates with the history of theories of the sublime. In the eighteenth century, the high point of such theory in Europe, arguably the most important literary source for examples was Milton's *Paradise Lost* (see Kirwan 50–51). Edmund Burke, for instance, singles out the great poet's description of the "travels of the fallen angels through their dismal habitation" (197). In *Observations on the Feeling of the Beautiful and Sublime* (1764), Kant also names among his examples "Milton's portrayal of the infernal kingdom" as something that arouses "enjoyment but with horror" (47). In focusing on the exit from Eden as the moment of glimpsing the sublime at the moment of loss, Justice takes advantage of the sublime potential of the story and the literary history that it bears.

As a critic concerned with the multiple effects of language, Justice wrote in the tradition of Longinus, whom he refers to, for example, in his essay "The Prose Sublime" (1998a, 43). Longinus (or Pseudo-Longinus) is the figure with whom the term *sublime* is most readily associated. As G. M. A. Grube explains in his translator's introduction to Longinus's treatise, the text that generally goes by the title *On the Sublime* is better translated *On Great Writing*, for the treatise is of such general scope as to take in several forms of great writing, not merely the "grand style," of the ancient world. Harold Bloom maintains that the work's title might also be translated *On Strong Poetry* or *On Literary Strength* (1987, 59). Although Longinus lists five "sources most productive of great writing"—such as "vigor of mental conception" and "dignified and distinguished word-arrangement" (10)—he sums up the tenor of his study when he points out that "great writing is the echo of a noble mind" (12). The ethos of the writer (or orator), the manifestation of a noble mind, is thus the true source of strong poetry. Related to the creation of this ethos is Longinus's emphasis on the importance of the great writers of the past when carrying out one's literary labors—the importance, for example, of asking, "How would these words of mine strike Homer or Demosthenes?" (23).

Longinus's insight that great writing of the present must be in dialogue with great writing of the past anticipates, at least remotely, T. S. Eliot's "Tradition and the Individual Talent." As Dana Gioia notes in his aptly titled "Tradition and an Individual Talent," Justice's poems often "originate out of other literary texts" (CS 67), thus participating in a kind of dialogue with them. While much the same can be said of virtually any poetry worth considering, Gioia's emphasis is that Justice practices a "full disclosure" in his literary borrowings and influences that is unusual among American poets. In his efforts to make something new, Justice was always looking to examples of the past, though he never—at least in the work he was willing to release for publication—merely imitated. He wrote, in other words, in the company of the great poets of several traditions without forgetting the date on the calendar. As in his critical work—in which he wrote in dialogue with such figures as Longinus, Coleridge, Eliot, John Crowe Ransom, and R. P. Blackmur (see Harp 1999), so in his poetry he wrote in dialogue with such precursors as Dante, Milton, Eliot, Stevens, and Baudelaire. This sense of tradition is central to the concern with the sublime. As Longinus emphasizes, having a strong tradition to draw on will assist one in the achievement of great writing. For Justice's sense of the sublime as sublime erasure, one must have a long tradition of sources of the sublime to glimpse in their passing. The erasure and the passing are different views of the same moment.

As noted at the beginning of this chapter, some reviewers of Justice's work concede his expertise as a technician of verse while maintaining that it lacks the stuff of greatness. Perhaps the most obvious, and the best, response to this criticism is that made already by other reviewers (for example, Nemerov and Elliott)—that much more is going on in these poems than the technical perfection that may have proved distracting to some readers. I should also like to emphasize that the devotion to technique, which is often a "love that masquerades as pure technique" ("Nostalgia of the Lakefronts," CP 222), is precisely what allows Justice to transform and bring to life what he calls up from tradition. His devotion to technique is deeply related to his devotion to the depersonalization of art—for technique is one of his prime depersonalizing mechanisms—but he is also writing out of his own experience. Part of this experience is the feel for the texts that gave rise to certain poems—the experience of the literary texts that were important parts of his life. But often another important part of this experience is what Justice brings to the poem outside of his reading—his own moments of growing up, seeing the world change, and confronting the deaths of friends. At the same time, the creation of art was also for him a process of distancing himself from his own experience. As he has said, "I want to treat the personal stuff as impersonally as if I were making it all up" (2001, 45). It is the distancing, depersonalizing function of technique that makes the experience available to the reader. This devotion to technique also allows Justice to risk so much to nostalgia; the human longing for a home that never was becomes all the more poignant and real for the reader because of the objectifying technique, which gives form and structure to the nostalgia. This complex sense of nostalgia relates also to the sublime, for the latter is what can exist in Justice's poems only in the past tense. The moment of glimpsing both the lost home and the sublime involves the realization that they are lost and that, in fact, in their most idealized forms, they never were.

Another important characteristic of the sublime is terror experienced at some remove from immediate danger. In *A Philosophical Enquiry into the Sublime and the Beautiful* (1757), Edmund Burke emphasizes that the "passions which belong to self-preservation," painful when the subject is in real danger, are "delightful when we have an idea of pain and danger, without being actually in such circumstances" (97). It is this sense of the sublime that Kant takes up in *Critique of Judgement* (1790) and associates with humans' supersensible "vocation" (see 92, 99, and passim), the calling to rise through reason above the immediate dictates of the senses to the level of "higher faculties of cognition" (123). For the sublime does not exist, for the Kant of the third critique, in the things observed—"the boundless ocean rising with rebellious force, the high waterfall of some mighty river, and the like" (91)— but rather in the capacity of the human mind to resist the immediate sense of threat and to view and experience these things in accordance with such higher faculties as reason and judgment. The source of the sublime, then, is the human mind itself. The object being viewed becomes "sublime because the mind has been incited to abandon sensibility" (76). Kant is focusing here on the sublime in nature, but insofar as experiences of art invoke, at a further remove, similar feelings and similarly set in motion one's higher faculties, it is fair to include art in Kant's view of humans' supersensible, or intellectual, vocation. For Justice, as for many artists, art is as intellectual a vocation as any other.

This idea of the sublime is quite complicated in relationship to Justice's "The Wall"; to begin with, it is complicated because the reader experiences the sublime moment at a double remove. If art already represents the sublime object—that upon which the human mind performs its work—at a distance, then the distance is doubled in the case of "The Wall," for the reader encounters the sublime moment not only virtually through the poem, but also vicariously through the figures of Adam and Eve. Further, what Johnson emphasized with regard to *Paradise Lost* may be applied to the human figures of Justice's sonnet as well—that they are undergoing something removed from any familiar world of human experience. The exit from the garden at the end of the poem is precisely the moment of transition from myth into history. This movement into history is also the exact moment in which the two catch a glimpse of the sublime that signals their, and by extension the reader's, intellectual and spiritual vocation. The glimpse of the sublime and the sublime fading occur as necessary parts of the same moment. This loss and the following movement into history are the prices of their glimpse of the sublime, and yet it is this very glimpse that sets them in motion in a more complex world. Experiencing this moment at several removes, the reader catches a glimpse already in a state of alienation.

In "The Sublime and the Avant-Garde," Jean-François Lyotard emphasizes the sublime as that which evades expectation, which moves into a realm of the event, the occurrence that stands apart from and resists repetition of the same; it is what "dismantles consciousness, what deposes consciousness . . . what consciousness cannot formulate, and even what consciousness forgets in order to constitute itself" (197). The moment of Justice's sonnet formulates the realm of the event, locating itself in the transition from the world of sheer sameness and repetition into the world beyond the wall, the world where the event, the unexpected, becomes possible. The enclosed world of Eden no longer exists, and the world beyond the wall is not yet, has not yet become constitutive of human experience; this moment exemplifies the impossible, for human consciousness cannot formulate the moment both before history begins and after the Edenic wholeness has broken down. The poem thus formulates entry into the event. The sublime unfurling marks this transition after the breakdown of mythic consciousness and before the full entry into historical-mindedness, though the latter already exists as a result of the breakdown of the former. History is yet to be made, but it is already in the making.

Lyotard goes on to stress that what was beginning to happen in Longinus's treatise, with its emphasis on the indeterminate moment of the sublime, is a movement toward a conception of rhetoric that disrupts the rules of a given school or discipline. The sublime style knows when to disregard the old rules for the sake of the grandeur it pursues. Further, in moving away from the familiar decorum in its deployment of tropes and figures of speech, a sublime style becomes ironically available in withholding assent to the traditional rules, and even in silence. Revealing with regard to this issue of silence and withholding are Lyotard's comments on Boileau's translation of Longinus: "What can remain of rhetoric (or of poetics) when the rhetorician in Boileau's translation announces that to attain the sublime effect 'there is no better figure of speech than one which is completely hidden, that which we do not even recognize as a figure of speech?' Must we admit that there are techniques for hiding figures, that there are figures for the erasure of figures?" (201). Such figures of erasure can be found in Justice's poems. The remainder of Lyotard's essay locates the sublime in the moment of privation when so much of the European world, under the influence of the "metaphysics of capital, which is a technology of time," has come to expect constant change and innovation. In such a context, the sublime becomes the "undoing of the presumption of the mind with respect to time" (211). The sublime is thus the moment of erasure in the face of the expectation of more.

The book of Justice's that most emphasizes such erasure is *Departures* (1973) (see chapter 4), but the sensibility that produced this later book was already under formation at the time of *The Summer Anniversaries*. To bring this sensibility into sharper relief, I leap ahead a bit by quoting "From a Notebook," which appears in *Departures*:

> G. maintains that the Adjective somehow penetrates the Noun with all that is most private, thereby becoming the most Personal of the Parts of Speech, hence the most Beautiful.
>
> I, on the contrary, maintain that the Conjunction, being Impersonal, is the more Beautiful, and especially when suppressed. (CP 150–51)

Here we encounter not only a statement of Justice's commitment to depersonalization, but also his commitment to objective distance and the virtues of erasure. The impersonal and objective are most beautiful, especially when they remain unstated. As Lyotard points out, there are indeed "figures for the erasure of figures"; the trick is to find the formulation that enables such suppression, such erasure as shimmers with absence, something undisclosed. The simple blank page will not do; for the beautiful and the sublime to be experienced as suppressed, there must be figures to create the effect of erasure. For example, behind Justice's sonnet stands the grand language and imagery of *Paradise Lost*, and behind both stands the Genesis story with its "flaming sword which turned every way, to guard the way to the tree of life" (3:24). By suggesting just enough and leaving out the rest, "The Wall" invokes these grand figures while allowing them to remain absent from the poem; the sublime, if seen at all, can only be glimpsed, and then only in passing. In the spirit of Kant's analysis, the cognitive functions, including the artistic pursuits, set into motion by this glimpse signal the vocation of the human intellect on the move.

Matthew Arnold (149–60; see also Ryle and Soper 1–19) noted that encounters with the sublime have an important function in the formation of a cultured person. While Justice was never one to write didactic poetry, "The

Wall" nevertheless impresses upon the reader—at least upon this reader—a complex view of the world in which humans, bearing some fragment of a sublime vision, set out to negotiate the ambiguities of history. As Berryman said of the poem, "It makes a *very* nice impression."

The poem that follows "The Wall" in *The Summer Anniversaries*, "A Dream Sestina" (CP 14–15), continues into the ambiguous realm of history, though in relation to a decidedly Dantesque landscape. Justice reported (CS 186) that he dreamed the first eleven lines of this poem—which explains both the title and why the word order is slightly out of joint. Given the end words of the first stanza of this sestina, the final two end words of the second stanza should be *faces* (line 5) followed by *circle* (line 6), instead of the other way around. In the sestina form, each stanza following the first should repeat the end words of the previous stanza in the following order: 6–1–5–2–4–3. Performing this same operation on the sixth and final stanza (I am leaving the three-line envoy out of consideration here) should yield the same word order as the opening stanza; however, this order does not work out in the present case. Thus, the sestina is slightly skewed, a condition that works well as a marker of the process of composition, one in which the dream work has yielded a fragment for the poet to work out. The result is a vision of the world that gestures toward something of Dante's attempt at a comprehensive system, but with a flaw (the skewed order of end words) that marks the brokenness of the old symmetries and points toward the fragments that remain.

The "Dream Sestina" as a whole takes much of its imagery from the opening of Dante's *Inferno*. For example, the opening stanza—with its "wood," "hill," and "circle"—recalls the situation at the opening of Dante's poem, in which "Dante" (the character in the poem rather than the historical personage) reports having lost his way in life:

In the middle of our life's way,
I came to myself in a dark wood
because the true way was lost. (canto 1, lines 1–3)

The final line of Justice's opening stanza—"I knew that I had lost my way"—echoes Dante's third line, though with the emphasis on the personal path ("my way") in isolation, rather than Dante's emphasis on his having strayed from the "true way" ("*diritta via*")—the universal way for all. In Justice's poem there is no true and universal way, so there is no assurance of a universal path to return to. He further stresses the personal isolation by the dream setting, for the darkness and woods belong to the unconscious of the isolated, dreaming psyche. The stresses that are confronted by this troubled psyche are those of history, after the Garden is lost.

The sestina holds out some hope of community, but this hope turns out to be in vain, for the "friends" whom the dreamer encounters turn out to be neither helpful nor friendly. By the third stanza, they have become like trees, a "human wood," unresponsive to the dreamer's questions. This human wood is also a remote echo of Dante's *Inferno*—Canto 13, where the poet encounters souls of the dead trapped inside of trees. At least in Dante's version, the figure of the poet is able to engage one of these souls, Pier della Vigna, in dialogue. In Justice's version, the "friends" merely stare "like blocks of wood," and while they do discuss him—"but not like friends"—they never address him directly. They treat him like an object, refusing to acknowledge his subjectivity.

Finally, like "Dante" on his pilgrimage, the figure of the poet in Justice's sestina moves in circles. In the *Inferno*, however, these circular movements —which are not precise circles, which would simply repeat themselves—spiral in a slow though real progression. And while they move closer and closer to the depths of Hell, they are also moving, through the progression of the entire *Divine Comedy*, closer and closer to the beatific vision. In "A Dream Sestina," the circles—the circle of friends, the "lone bird wheeling in a circle," the "fiery circle" that is the sun—promise no progress. The one moment that seems to hold out some promise of escape comes in response to the horrific "trees with human faces":

> Afraid, I ran a little way
> But must have wandered in a circle.

Yet again, this is a circle that turns back on itself rather than a spiral that promises some progression. The only way out of this nightmare vision is to awaken from the poem.

Much of the remainder of *The Summer Anniversaries* dwells in realms more of history than of myth. Several of the poems explore the poet's southern roots, the particular strain of history into which Justice was born, though his South was quite different from the one he had read about in William Faulkner. The title of another of Justice's sonnets, "Southern Gothic" (CP 22), is one that might be more readily associated with Faulkner. As it turns out, the sonnet has more to disclose about Justice's distance from the southern gothic tradition than about his association with it. The poem bears the dedication "for W.E.B & P.R." These two dedicatees, Edgar Bowers and Paul

Ramsey, are fitting for this poem meditating on the speaker's relationship to a southern tradition, for they are "Southern poets and friends from Chapel Hill days."[4] The sonnet takes up one of Justice's recurring themes—the encounter with fragments left over from a past seemingly much grander than the present:

> Something of how the homing bee at dusk
> Seems to inquire, perplexed, how there can be
> No flowers here, not even withered stalks of flowers,
> Conjures a garden where no garden is
> And trellises too frail almost to bear
> The memory of a rose, much less a rose.

The single bee cuts a rather forlorn figure. Classically, bees are associated with growing and flourishing civilization, as in Virgil's *Aeneid*, where bees become the figure for Queen Dido's men laboring to build a new civilization from the ground up:

> The bees, throughout the blooming countryside,
> thus labor in the early summer, leading
> the newly grown into the sun, or press
> their liquid honey into cells that stretch
> with that sweet nectar, or accept the burdens
> that workers bring, or like an army drive
> along the drones, that lazy crew; the work
> is shining, honey redolent of thyme. (bk. 1, lines 430–36)[5]

By contrast, the single bee in Justice's poem, in search of what it cannot find, becomes a figure of the speaker's own alienation and sense of loss. The bee seems to have appeared after the work of a civilization is over. What the speaker finds to support his imagination are frail trellises indeed, too frail to hold up a rose, though just sufficient to bear the weight of a rose unfolding in memory only. Although the poem includes monumental oaks, what they shade is a mere fragment of the past, a "house of broken windows merely/And empty nests up under broken eaves." All is emptiness and loss. The scene sounds southern gothic enough, but it is a scene merely; no tale unfolds. There is no Quentin Compson to tell the tale, nor a Henry Sutpen (as in Faulkner's *Absalom, Absalom!*—the end of which Justice would later use as an epigraph to his poem "My South," which appears in *The Sunset Maker* [1987]) living upstairs, waiting to die. The only roses left, besides those in memory and imagination, are those represented on the peeling wallpaper inside the house, where the damask "unravels, peeling from a wall, / Red roses within roses within roses."

Earlier I associated Justice's image of the rose with Dante's grand vision of the faithful near the end of the *Paradiso*, which echoes in Justice's work as a remnant of a grand past. A version of the image also occurs in one of his more proximate precursors, T. S. Eliot. Justice may not have necessarily had these references explicitly in mind when he wrote, but they point toward a great store of images and associations from which he freely, if at times unconsciously, drew. Certainly, Dante and Eliot are poets whom he admired, so it makes sense to trace some of the influence of their work where doing so helps to illuminate Justice's writing. One might think, for example, of Eliot's "Rose of memory / Rose of Forgetfulness" (1962, 87–88) in section two of his penitential poem "Ash-Wednesday," which calls attention to the fallenness and fragmentation of the world. Other roses that appear in Eliot's poems, such as the "Multifoliate rose" of "The Hollow Men" (81), also recall the passage from *Paradiso* (Canto 31) that I quoted earlier. There is a remote echo of this visionary moment at the end of Eliot's *Four Quartets*, where the "fire and the rose are one" (209). But this moment in Eliot exists only in anticipation, for his meditation on time, history, and longing for the divine can only anticipate such a vision as Dante formulates at the end of his great poem.

In Justice's "Southern Gothic," the rose image echoes most faintly through Eliot back to Dante's grand vision, which Justice's poem finally refuses, albeit with admiration. The latter-day roses are indeed multifoliate, for they are "roses within roses within roses," though they are red rather than the white of Dante's mystical rose—not the color of the blessed in the hereafter, but rather that of the blood of history, the blood that will flow through Justice's poem "The Assassination" (see chapter 4). Further, these latter-day multifoliate roses are merely the wallpaper designs that once decorated the house; they are all that is left of Dante's vision, as the house is all that is left of a Faulknerian vision of the southern past. But this imagery of the faded roses of history remains and even suffices for the work of art. Here, what redemption there is comes through art.

"Beyond the Hunting Woods" (CP 24), which is set in a similar after time, explores another ruin, this one of a "great house" that is "Turreted and towered / In nineteenth-century style." The "Odor of jessamine / And roses, canker-bit," recall, in Proustian fashion,

            famous times
When dame and maiden sipped
Sassafras or wild
Elderberry wine,
While far in the hunting woods
Men after their red hounds
Pursued the mythic beast.

The scene of the "great house/Beyond the hunting woods," along with the hunters pursuing the "mythic beast," calls up another association with Faulkner, this one connected to his novella *The Bear* (1961), which concerns the waning of a culture centered on the relationship between the grand civilities of the house and town and the savagery of the woods, the latter of which is embodied in the semimythic bear, Old Ben, that the narrator, Ike Mc-Caslin, finally glimpses while under the tutelage of Sam Fathers, who, as his name implies, carries knowledge of the old ways. Ike McCaslin's generation is the last to experience the woods as an enveloping wilderness. The death of Old Ben corresponds with the death of the wilderness as truly wild, along with the way of life represented by the hunting camp and the communion with the wilderness to which it is devoted. When this latter life dies, so does the grand civilization of the town, for the two have a deep and reciprocal relationship. Justice's poem takes up the experience of a subsequent genera-tion, to whom this former life is not even a remote memory, but rather a distant rumor. If the language here creaks a bit with an archaic-sounding formality, the slight clumsiness is at the service of evoking the world that is already absent. It is only "of a stranger" that this speaker can ask why it is that the old world vanished, for surely no one in the speaker's familiar world would know. But no answer is forthcoming. As with "Southern Gothic," this poem pays tribute to as well as sets a seal on a cultural moment and a liter-ary mode no longer available.

    The poem that ends section one of *The Summer Anniversaries*, "Tales from a Family Album" (CP 25–26), also takes up the scene of a diminished pres-ent from which a grand past is recalled. Here the point of reference creates a sweep into the ancient world, for as the speaker points out,

No house of Atreus ours, too humble surely,
The family tree a simple chinaberry
Such as springs up in Georgia in a season.

The reference to the house of Atreus, the focus of Aeschylus's trilogy *The Or-esteia*, raises an important set of associations for the poem. As Robert Fagles and W. B. Stanford emphasize in their introduction to the play, "No other Greek family can rival" the house of Atreus "for accumulated atrocities" (14). And yet the tragedy takes us from the savagery of Agamemnon's slaughter of his daughter Iphigeneia, as well as Clytemnestra's slaughter of Agamemnon, to the relative harmony of a civilization that has found a way to keep its destructive impulses in check. We thus journey, through the trilogy, from the Watchman's pained anticipation at the beginning of *Agamemnon* to the Athenian women's concluding song in *The Eumenides*, where "All-seeing Zeus and Fate embrace" (277). "Tales from a Family Album" takes us to a much later moment that is less grand but also less savage, though this later world has troubles enough.

While Justice creates a lightly comic tone with his literalizing of the family tree to a chinaberry, he also introduces into the poem a struggle for harmony among competing forces—those of civilization and savagery, which remain in tension here even if they lack the epic scope of the house of Atreus. They are, like the chinaberry, humble and close to the earth—the earth not of myth but of everyday life. Nevertheless, there is something in the family appearance "bespeaking an acquaintance, / not casual and not recent, with a monster." No sooner do we hear of this "monster," however, than its stature is diminished by a loose association with the creature that the speaker's aunt kept "in shape of a green parrot." The monster that haunts the family would seem to be imaginary. In fact, the speaker goes on to recount an uncle who told stories "Touching that beast, wholly imaginary, / Which, hunting once, his hounds had got the wind of." Even if this beast is the product of an imaginary tale, it nevertheless informs the speaker's sense of his family's identity as touched with something alien and troubling. Further, there is a cousin on "whom the mark is printed of a forepaw." The mark suggests that there may be something to these family stories after all, though one need not rely on tales of monsters to explain such a mark. Like the aunt's "monster" in the shape of a parrot, this paw print may yield to a wholly naturalistic explanation. The natural world need not be a Faulknerian enveloping wilderness to hold out dangers.

Nor need we revert to the grand and dangerous figures of Aeschylus's writing, or even of Faulkner's, to confront the real hazards of the human world. The second-to-last verse paragraph of the poem comes closest to suggesting a psychological explanation for the stories alluded to. From his childhood the speaker recalls a relative "who died young, though as a hag most toothless." This relative's hair had turned "wintry" from an encounter with a stranger in the woods. The story implies some violence in the encounter, though the assaulting stranger "had as well been unicorn or centaur / For all she might recall of him thereafter." The association with the centaur implies a story of violence, for—excepting Chiron, the most gentlemanly of the centaurs—they were a rapacious lot. The poem's implicit impulse to mythologize functions in part as a way of emotionally distancing and transforming what seems too difficult to confront in its literal and violent details. But presumably this "stranger" is a human being who has done violence to the speaker's relative. I take it that this is merely one example of the savagery that any family, indeed any person, living in the world must learn to confront; such are the implications of this family's album. Even if the literal details of the violence are concealed in mythologized versions, the impulse to mythologize, to tell stories, assures that some version of what happened will be passed along. The truth will out, even if only in transformed and encoded versions.

The final verse paragraph confronts this difficulty of finding an adequate code for the communication of one's stories. The speaker informs us of another relative who "took up pen and paper / To write our history, whereat he perished." The history proves to be untellable, at least by this relative. In the telling of a family's history, much depends on what one means by the telling of the story. One who would set out to write a truly definitive version of anything—if "definitive" is to mean a version that precludes ever having anything further to say on the matter—is doomed to failure. Because there is never really a single statement to be made about anything, and because it is impossible ever truly to exhaust all possibilities (for our endings are always provisional), there is a strong sense in which all human discourse is fundamentally fragmentary—as is this present statement about the genre of the fragment. These observations are relevant to the work of Justice, who stated: "Fragments appeal to me—there's an inevitable pathos about them. Which may be an unacknowledged reason for the appeal of so much that's chaotic in art nowadays, unfinished" (PS 41). The artfully handled fragment can stimulate the reader's imagination to enter into the realm of the art. While the fragment can become an instrument of nostalgia, Justice's mode of reflective nostalgia makes the fragment part of a continuing process of making new uses of old materials (see Tracy 1999a and 1999b). The way that Justice chooses for this poem, getting at the complexities of a family's history, as well as the complexities of this history's tellings and withholdings, is quite compelling.

The poem "Thus" (CP 29), which opens section two of *The Summer Anniversaries*, provides a kind of ars poetica for a mode of suggestive understatement. It voices devotion to an art of a minor key in which even the "major resolution of the minor, / . . . would be too noble." In his art the speaker will see to it that the "variations / Keep faith with the plain statement of the oboe." The mention of the oboe is significant for Justice's poetry. In the Romantic era, given the oboe's conventional association with pastoral, it aroused "nostalgia for an idealized past" (Burgess and Haynes 215). Oscar Comettant (1820–98) wrote of the instrument's effects that the "soul becomes sick from that mysterious illness, that mix of happiness, sadness, regret, hope and love that is called nostalgia" (quoted in ibid., 221). The oboe was used in *Orphée* for the "echo of Euridice's voice rising from the Underworld" and in "*Alceste* where Alceste remembers her children" (ibid., 225). In the traditional stream of the twentieth century, the instrument continued to be conventionally associated with melancholy and alienation. It did not come to be much associated with avant-garde experimentation until the 1970s (ibid., 240–45, 267). With the poem's emphasis on the "plain statement of the oboe" and each string repeating the lesson "without overmuch adornment," Justice's "Thus" signals devotion to a plain statement of complex emotions. The plain statement of the fragment performs epic labor in Justice's poetry.

Like "A Dream Sestina," "Women in Love" (CP 34) draws on Dante's work. A modified villanelle—composed of thirteen rather than nineteen lines—the poem makes explicit reference to its precursor:

> Their choice of hells would be the one they know.
> Dante describes it, the wind circling there.
> The knack is this, to fasten and not let go.

The circling wind and the fastening and not letting go call to mind Canto 5 of the *Inferno*, where "Dante" and "Virgil" encounter Paolo and Francesca, eternally bound together and blown around by the wind among the other figures who subjugate reason to appetite. Because Justice once commented to me that the translation of the *Inferno* he preferred was Longfellow's, I quote from the early American poet's version:

> The infernal hurricane that never rests
> Hurtles the spirits onward in its rapine;
> Whirling them round, and smiting, it molests them. (lines 31–33)

Those condemned to this, the second circle of the Inferno, have made a definite decision, and thus their wills loom much larger than the rather diminished figures in Justice's poem, who more resemble the hapless spirits of Dante's Canto 3, those outside the City of Dis proper. These are the souls who refused to make any commitment, either to good or to evil; lacking all conviction, they are kept away from the truly damned because in the presence of these shriveled souls, the damned—who at minimum had the courage of their disordered convictions—would be proud. As Dante comments, "Misericord [Mercy] and Justice both disdain them" (canto 5, line 50). Justice writes of the figures in his poem, "Desire is limbo—they're unhappy there." This "limbo" is not the technical "Limbo," the *limbus patrum* where, as traditionally conceived, the "pious heathen had to await the opening of heaven by Christ" (Rahner and Vorgrimler 262), but rather the border or liminal space of estrangement where these figures pass their lives of alienation; it is perhaps a state of life that Justice saw many condemned to in the culture of mid-twentieth-century America.

As signaled by his poem "Thus," Justice's work is a study in plain statement and understatement, in which he skillfully modulates tone in his responses to the tradition that he has assembled for himself, as Eliot said that a poet must do (1960, 4–7). As stated above, Dana Gioia has indicated how often Justice consciously confronted and even named the precursor text that he was using (CS 67); however, he was also quite capable of making unconscious use of precursor texts. A notable example is "The Stray Dog by the Summerhouse" (CP 41–42) as a response to Richard Eberhart's "The Groundhog," which was first published in 1934 in the British literary weekly the *Listener* (Roache 111) and was included in Eberhart's book *Reading the Spirit* (1936). The example is notable as an *unconscious* response to a precursor poem because Justice once commented to me that when he wrote the poem, he did not have Eberhart's example in mind. If there is a subgenre of the dead animal poem in twentieth-century American poetry, then Eberhart's "The Groundhog" may well be the exemplar text. Justice's response is noteworthy for the subtlety of its modulations.

"The Groundhog" features several visits to the dead animal's decaying carcass until it has disappeared altogether. Through much of the poem, as the speaker seeks to avoid the significance of what he observes, he remains in "intellectual chains" by casting his observations in strikingly abstract terms, for example:

Inspecting close his maggots' might
And seething cauldron of his being.

In Eberhart's belatedly Romantic mode, this decay and disappearance finally break into a meditation on the fate of civilization:

> I stood there in the whirling summer,
> My hand capped a withered heart,
> And thought of China and of Greece,
> Of Alexander in his tent;
> Of Montaigne in his tower,
> Of Saint Theresa in her wild lament.

Cleanth Brooks (28–29) pointed out that these three figures at the end—the man of action, the detached intellectual, and the mystic—exemplify different attitudes toward death. At a reading at the University of Florida in the fall of 1989, Eberhart himself explained, in similar terms, that these closing lines express his philosophy of life, with the three figures at the end standing, in ascending order, for three approaches to life. The charismatic figure of Alexander occupies the lowest order because, although he might have been a fascinating character to know, his life's work was based on killing. Montaigne, the figure of intellectual achievement, remains on the second level because of his detachment from the world in his tower. Saint Theresa as the embodiment of the mystic or saint stands on the highest level for Eberhart. Further, this figure of the saint in the throes of her mystical passion is the one best prepared for the world's dissolution, represented by the decaying body of the groundhog.

Justice's contribution to the subgenre of the dead animal poem is at once more circumstantial and more detached, as well as noteworthy for the absence of any overt, overarching vision. To say as much is not to assert that the poem bears "no suggestion of a complete world-picture," nor that there is "no moral structure behind or beneath the surface" of the poem, as Justice had written in response to his friend Richard Stern's poems years earlier (see chapter 1). Rather, Justice's poem does its work of suggesting a world picture more subtly than Eberhart's marvelously over-the-top example. Justice's speaker implies his solidarity with a fellow creature by describing its body in stark and affectionate detail:

> This morning, down
> By the summerhouse,
> I saw a stray,
> A stray dog dead.
> All white and brown
> The dead friend lay,
> All brown with a white
> Mark on his head.

He then describes the "worms inside" the body—an echo of Eberhart's "maggots' might," though with the difference that it is more specific than the abstract noun "might" modified by the plural possessive "maggots'." Justice's poem remains focused on the details of this "dead friend" being reclaimed by the earth in a process of decay that produces a "sweet" smell like that of a "round, ripe pear" that

> Had dropped to the ground
> And with the heat
> Was turning black.

Part of what reinforces this focus on detail is the shortness of the lines—predominantly iambic dimeter—such that generally each line carries a single image or detail. Further, although there is no regular rhyme scheme, each end word echoes with at least one other; these echoes range from the repetition of an entire word ("butterflies") to off-rhyme (for example, "summerhouse" and "loose"). But then the final eight lines, which articulate the comparison between the smell of the decaying "friend" and the overripe pear, resolve into a controlled rhyme scheme beginning with an off-rhyme couplet ("near" and "pear") followed by a perfectly rhymed couplet ("round" and "ground") followed by four lines rhyming a–b–b–a. This resolution into a recognizable pattern of rhyme reinforces the poem's sense of control and restraint as it closes on a note of peaceful resignation that takes its cue from the congruence of the decaying body and the smell of overripe fruit. What grows out of the earth is fertilized by what has died and returned to the earth, as what becomes ripe quickly becomes overripe—like the pear described in the simile. The speaker acknowledges the process of which he is a part, implicitly acknowledging that the earth will claim him, too.

With "Anthony St. Blues" (CP 43), Justice paid tribute to T. S. Eliot, whose urban portraits "Preludes" and "Rhapsody on a Windy Night" loom behind the poem. Again, part of what sets Justice's poem apart from its precursors is its more circumstantial presentation of a world:

> Morning. The roofs emerge, the yard—
> Brown grass, puddled with snow, dog's bone—
> Emerges slowly, but not yet
> Her plumber from the widow's arms,
> To touch his dreaming truck awake
> That all night slumbered by our curb . . .

The plumber provides a striking point of contrast to Eliot's more impressionistic poems, in which we never learn what anyone in these cityscapes does for a living. Just enough of the scene is filled out in Justice's poem to create a sense of a somewhat dreary everyday world—what with the brown grass, the snow puddle, and the early-morning departure for work—that these characters must negotiate. But there is also a hint of intrigue, for the plumber seems to have spent the night with a widow, a somewhat risqué detail for 1960. In the trajectory of *The Summer Anniversaries* as a whole, this poem punctuates the overall movement from the earlier and at times mythic poems of loss to a more fully realized historical world with its jobs and daily round. In the latter poems, the sense of loss is a foregone conclusion. Having followed the book's movement into this thoroughly historical realm, the reader confronts studies of the torments of everyday life:

> The one-armed man, returning late,
> Bends to retrieve the murderous news,
> Tucks it beneath the willing stump,
> And mounts once more with slippery care
> The purgatory of the stoop.

Eden is not a possibility for this figure, nor are the extremes of Hell. Rather, his is the in-between realm of an everyday purgatory that—unlike the cleansing realm of Dante—promises no purgation followed by an entry into heaven. The only hint of news is "murderous," and while the man's loss of an arm could hint at some violent or adventurous past, he is now left with only the "willing stump" under which he carries the bad news inside.

"A Winter Ode to the Old Men of Lummus Park, Miami, Florida" (CP 44) brings an intimation of the land of the dead into the world of history:

> Risen from rented rooms, old ghosts
> Come back to haunt our parks by day,
> They crept up Fifth Street through the crowd,
> Unseeing and almost unseen,
> Halting before the shops for breath . . .

The speaker treats these old ghosts, who are also humans living in the world, with a reverential detachment, puzzling through metaphors by which to understand them: "A little thicket of thin trees" and "wan heliotropes." They are, in other words, parts of nature seeking sustenance from the sun. When he addresses them directly in the second verse paragraph, he takes a cue from his earlier image of the heliotrope, a plant that follows the light of the heat-giving sun, but then shifts to a metaphor drawn from the realm of human instruments:

Poor cracked thermometers stuck now
At zero everlastingly.

That these men are figured in instrumental terms hints at an attitude of valuing them for their usefulness; and that they are stuck at zero indicates not only that they cannot get warm, but also that they have outlived their usefulness, leading to their marginalized existence. Their state of being stuck at zero "everlastingly" points to the zero at the bone that is the chill of their mortality.

The brief address to these "old ghosts" both pays tribute to them and apologizes for the treatment that has led to their diminished mode of existence:

Surely they must have thought you strong
To lean on you so hard, so long!

The act of leaning on these old men suggests treating them in the manner of crutches or canes, useful tools in making one's way. While the poem carries the suggestion that every generation must in some way depend on the generations of the past, it also suggests that it matters profoundly how a given generation does so.

One of Justice's more widely anthologized poems, "Counting the Mad" (CP 45), based on the structure of the children's rhyme "This Little Piggy," is a haunting treatment—after the manner of Elizabeth Bishop's "Visits to St. Elizabeth's"—of life in a mental institution. The opening line, "This one was put in a jacket," sounds innocuous enough except that given the title and the passive voice, one quickly realizes that "this one" is being restrained in a strait jacket. What follows is a litany of the activities of the troubled souls in this place, culminating in the obsessive cry of "No No No No." A hint of a turn occurs in the movement from line three to line four of the second stanza:

This one saw things that were not there,
This one things that were.

Troubling hallucinations are commonly enough associated with severe mental difficulties, but the juxtaposition of these two lines suggests that seeing things that are there might be as troubling as seeing things that are not.

This moment of stanza two prepares the way for the full turn of the third stanza:

This one thought himself a bird,
This one a dog,
And this one thought himself a man,
An ordinary man,
And cried and cried No No No No
All day long.

It is this everyday life, within which this figure thinks himself an "ordinary man," that proves to be most disconcerting, and which provokes his all-day-long refusal. As Walker Percy wrote about throughout his career, the great hardship that human beings share is the burden of dragging our ambiguous and uncertain selves through the world. Although Percy's, as well as Justice's, version of this story of human selfhood is inflected through existentialist and postexistentialist thought, it has a centuries-old provenance. Justice taps into this long tradition of associations. Erasmus, for example, in *The Praise of Folly*, alludes to the story of the Greek man who sat in a theater "for whole days on end, laughing, applauding, enjoying himself, because he thought that wonderful tragedies were being acted there, whereas nothing at all was being performed" (58–59). When his friends manage to effect a cure, the formerly deluded man takes them to task for depriving him of a "most pleasant delusion" (59). Clarence H. Miller points to Horace's Epistle 2.2 as Erasmus's likely source of this tale. However, another version of the story appears in the Pseudo-Aristotelian work "On Marvelous Things Heard": "It is said that a certain man in Abydos being deranged in mind, and going to the theatre on many days looked on (as though actors were performing a play), and applauded; and, when he was restored to his senses, he declared that that was the happiest time he had ever spent" (Aristotle 1276). One implication of these tales is that everyday life is a kind of madness, the cure for which is folly and delusion. In Justice's "Counting the Mad," the man's realization that he is "ordinary" stands as itself a kind of sickness, reinforced by the syntactical structure, which parallels thinking oneself an "ordinary man" with thinking oneself a bird or a dog. The poem's speaker—a figure of the poet—stands apart from both the delusions and the ordinary everyday-ness, implying some possibility of avoiding both kinds of madness by means of art. If the artist cannot avoid everyday life entirely, he or she can at least stand a little apart.

Finally, the life of art is not an escape from everyday life, but rather a way of inhabiting the everyday with a spirit of detachment that enables critical and aesthetic distance. The question of how to inhabit everyday life also comes to the fore in the volume's final poem "To Satan in Heaven" (CP 48), a thoroughly Baudelairian poem, though not a direct imitation, such as "The Metamorphoses of a Vampire" (CP 55) (see Baudelaire's "Les Métamorphoses du Vampire"). The beginning of "To Satan in Heaven" seems straightforward enough in its request for forgiveness of "virtue's pedants," that is, those who make a show of their virtue: "keepers of promises" and "prizewinners." But then the speaker also asks forgiveness for "Our simple wish to be elsewhere" as well as for those (the members of Satan's party) who "Choose not to continue, the merely bored,/Who have modeled our lives after cloud-shapes." The irony here is that forgiveness is petitioned both for wishing to be elsewhere and for staying put and doing nothing but merely drifting, modeling existence on the motions of clouds. What possibility is left? I take it that the group for whom the poem speaks in its first-person plural is composed of those who wish to be elsewhere but who at the same time are not really present where they are; they do not really inhabit their lives but drift like clouds. In this regard they are not unlike those figures in the third canto of Dante's *Inferno*, who never committed themselves to good or to evil, but who drifted without commitment. They are, in the words of Justice's poem, "Meek as leaves in the wind's circus, evenings."

The irony that runs through the poem is the speaker's address of Satan as if the latter is the deity. I take this "Satan in Heaven" to be the fallen angel in a "heaven" of his own making, for at the end of the poem, the speaker asks for forgiveness for having

Reduced thee to our own scope and purpose,
Satan, who, though in heaven, downward yearned,
As the butterfly, weary of flowers,
Longs for the cocoon or the looping net.

Like the damned of the *Inferno*, Satan in this poem has the courage of his convictions and, longing to be elsewhere, has acted on his desire. Those for whom the poem speaks occupy the position of the souls not even allowed into the Inferno proper; meek souls blown about in their in-between state, they lack the substance even to choose evil.

In his modes of plain statement and understatement, Justice proceeds in dialogue with his tradition, creating fragments hearkening back to a grand and self-consciously idealized past but refusing to turn away from the ambiguities and the "boredom, and the horror, and the glory" of the present.

When the Justices' son, Nathaniel, was born—in August 1961—Donald wrote to Paul Engle: "We had a boy, born Thursday, after long hard labor on Jean's part and some anxiety on mine; I'm not quite recovered yet though she and the baby seem to be doing, as the saying goes, fine. . . . What with the excitements and distractions attendant on the event, I've put everything else aside for a while and am only just able to face other matters, such as correspondence." Some of these other matters had to do with the Writers' Workshop. In this same letter, he mentions his approval of having Robert Creeley come to teach as a visiting poet: "I don't myself believe in encouraging the usual run of beats but Creeley is not one of those though he is used by them as a good example. So it's fine with me to invite him."

The comment points to a recurring point of tension, for the workshop sometimes brought in visiting faculty whose styles clashed with Justice's preferences. His review "San Francisco and Palo Alto" (1958) stands as a helpful marker of his tastes and judgments around this time. In the title, San Francisco stands for the Beat poets Allen Ginsberg and Kenneth Patchen, Palo Alto for three former students of Yvor Winters at Stanford: Donald Drummond, Edgar Bowers, and Donald Hall—though as Justice points out, Hall's work in *Exiles and Marriages* is more difficult to classify. In the opening paragraph, the reviewer imagines "some clear-eyed reader of the future to whom these poems [Ginsberg's] will seem as quaint and old-fashioned as the senior Mr. Ginsberg's" (231)—that is, the famous poet's father, who also published verse. But then Justice also praises the closing line of "America" and the younger Ginsberg's sense of humor.

The clear preference, however, is for the "School of Palo Alto, of which [Yvor] Winters is the master and [J. V.] Cunningham the adept" (232). The approval is not without reservation, for Justice acknowledges the stultifying effect that adherence to an aesthetic program can have. He praises the poets for their ability to negotiate as well as escape their constraints. For example, he writes of Drummond's work in the following terms: "Iambic pentameter is both the glory and the bane of these poets. Recognizing it as part of the formula, Drummond shuns it in this, his second book, by adding extra feet or by dropping syllables to spring the rhythm: 'Oh, leave, leave, remit, consent, and leave!' (A tame rebellion, but a lovely line.)" (232). Although Justice in general modulates his tone rather carefully, there are moments when Ginsberg and Patchen come in for some vituperation. In a personal conversation with me, he recalled that when he discovered that he had greater facility in writing negative rather than positive reviews, he judged the reason to be a character flaw, so he decided to stop reviewing altogether.

The early 1960s saw the entry of Marvin Bell, Mark Strand, and Charles Wright as students into the workshop. Strand recalls that as a teacher Justice articulated his opinions clearly, though without trying to force his views. There was room for disagreement, but "it was always more fun to agree with Don, to enjoy a tacit sense of unity. Otherwise one felt on the wrong side, the side without standards" (CS 133–34). Strand describes the weekly meetings of the workshop, of which there was only one section at the time: "Don and Paul Engle ran the meetings. Paul was frequently called out of the room to answer the telephone or to run an urgent errand, which meant that Don did most of the actual teaching. Adding enough praise to keep his criticism from being harsh, he guided us through poems with a skill that was as painstaking as it was graceful" (ibid., 134). As Bell has pointed out: "Don put himself in the position of defending the poem against unwarranted criticisms. This did not mean that he himself necessarily thought highly of the poem. However, he was alert to each poem on its own terms and willing to defend it against criticisms based on irrelevant ideas."[1]

Justice's competitiveness, for which he was well known, also exerted an influence on the workshop culture. After workshop sessions, the drive to compete came out in ping-pong games at the student union. Strand recalls Justice's love of all kinds of games as outlets for the pressures of struggling to write good poetry. Bell makes a connection to the fact that "Don lost some of the playtime of his childhood to osteomyelitis. In adulthood, he loved games of all sorts, from poker to ping-pong, volleyball and softball, all of which he played with passion. One wondered if his enthusiasm for games had been strengthened by a need to make up for what he had missed."[2] Wright saw the gamesmanship as exerting a salutary influence on the students' work: "Competition. Much competition. It had a wonderful effect on one's poems. The push to get them written. The desire to get them written right for the proper praise from the proper people" (CS 139).

In 1964–65 the Justices lived in San Francisco, where Donald was a Ford Foundation Fellow in Theater at the Actor's Workshop. Without understanding why, he did not find life on the West Coast quite agreeable: "The enchantment of San Francisco hasn't ever quite taken hold on us. In fact for the last few weeks I've been quite depressed—only in the last few days do things (inwardly) seem to be improving. It's not the fault of the theater. Though I feel out of place there, it's an admirable company, and I expect to have learned quite a bit about theater from it. To tell you the truth, I don't know what it is—perhaps only vague urban pressures, after Iowa City quiet; and isolation, after community."[3] Even with the gloominess of his mood, the time at the theater company was productive; he wrote several poems, along with two short plays that the company directors were considering for performance. With Nathaniel spending mornings in nursery school, Jean was finding time to write as well.

In an essay about one of the poems that he wrote during this time ("Bus Stop"), Justice connected his feeling of displacement—according to which "I did not feel at all in possession of my own life" (PS 212)—with what was going on in the world:

> Certainly the world seemed that year on the point of conflagration. Gold-water bullies had roamed Nob Hill, our navy was attacked by phantoms in the Tonkin Gulf, Khrushchev fell, China exploded a nuclear device, the first defiant Berkeley students were dragged roughly down marble staircases, and at Thanksgiving General Taylor took off on his futile fact-finding mission to Vietnam. By late February the official bombing of North Vietnam had begun. The theater company was breaking up, and I fled the city. It sounds dramatic now, but it did feel that way at the time. (ibid., 215)

Nevertheless, the stay in San Francisco had its pleasant side also, such as the "exemplary view" that their rented house afforded, though "in a dark mood it could leave you feeling remote and isolated" (ibid., 210).

Every evening Justice walked their dog, Hugo. During these walks he saw passengers getting off the buses that stopped at the bus stop near their house. The evening ritual led to the poem "Bus Stop" (CP 100), which considers

> The quiet lives
> That follow us—
> These lives we lead
> But do not own—
>
> Stand in the rain
> So quietly

When we are gone,
So quietly . . .

The speaker and those for whom he speaks in the first-person plural—for
here the only community available to the rather isolated speaker is the virtual one he implies with this pronoun—are alienated from their very existen-
ces. The poem plays on the idea of these people *leading* their lives, taking up
the implication that their lives must therefore be *following* them, meaning
that they and their lives exist separately. Further, it is difficult not to hear in
this poem's reiteration of "So quietly" echoes of Thoreau's famous observation that the "mass of men lead lives of quiet desperation" (7), for there is an
aura of muted desperation in this poem's description of figures in the rain.

The arrival of the bus leads to a subtly dramatic moment:

And the last bus
Comes letting dark
Umbrellas out—
Black flowers, black flowers.

The identification of the bus as the evening's last brings a hint of urgency
into the scene, for something is ending here. There is also a moment of
arrival as the passengers step into the rain. In his essay Justice makes an
apt observation concerning the image of the passengers getting off the bus
and opening their black umbrellas one after another: "I sensed something
symbolic in this, as if centuries hence it might be recalled as part of an
ancient urban ritual whose meaning had been forgotten. And vividly there
rose up before me a picture of the raised umbrellas which had represented
the dead in the last scene of *Our Town*, called back now from the pages,
years before, of *Life* magazine" (PS 210–11). The connection to the final scene
of Thornton Wilder's *Our Town*—where the dead sit impassively talking
among themselves from their places in the graveyard, waiting for whatever
is to come—combined with the allusion to Thoreau's diagnosis of quiet desperation and the speaker's own sense of separation from life, implies that
these figures are walking in the midst of a living death. This implication is
reinforced by the blossoming of the line "Black flowers, black flowers." In
the midst of this poem, with its four-syllable lines, each of which includes
two accented syllables (resolving for the most part into iambic dimeter), the
occurrence of this line of "black flowers"—whether it is to be read as two am-
phibrachic substitutions or as two elisions, with the two syllables of *flowers*
becoming one—brings emphasis to this dark flowering. This substitution or

elision serves a rhetorical function in calling attention to these black flowers that recall something of the sickly atmosphere of Baudelaire's *Les Fleurs du Mal*. At the very least, the lives of this poem are akin to the somnolent walkers whom Thoreau describes (67–68), leading to his anxiety about coming to die and discovering that he has not lived. That the poem's speaker includes himself among these figures makes the poem not an accusation, but rather an exploration of the quiet plangencies of this alienated existence.

The poem then allows a spark of optimism as the statement "And lives go on"—emphasizing sheer continuity—modulates into "And lives go on/Like sudden lights." If lives go on like lights, there is energy circulating in them still, though the mechanism of the lights going on implies that the lives, like the lights, may just as easily be switched off. On the other hand, as the final quatrain emphasizes, these lights may be "Left on for hours,/Burning, burning." The trochaic substitutions, which call extra attention to the line, and the repeated word serve to stress the sameness of these electrically burning lives; even if they are left on like lights, nothing much happens, only the expenditure of energy. The poem thus ends on a rather bleak note, a bleakness reinforced by the allusion—pointed out by Justice himself (PS 215)—to Saint Augustine's *Confessions*, in which "I came to Carthage, where a caldron of shameful loves seethed and sounded about me on every side" (77; bk. 3, ch. 1). Justice may also have had in mind the passage of *The Waste Land*—"To Carthage then I came / /Burning burning burning burning" (1962, 64)—that Eliot connected to the same passage in *The Confessions*. The atmosphere of "Bus Stop" is hardly so dire as Augustine's description of Carthage, or of much of Eliot's *Waste Land*, though the allusion gives weight to the idea that the surrounding culture lends little edification. But even with this bleak atmosphere, the poem is also a tribute to the simple endurance of going on day after day. The sense of tribute comes across in the extreme care of rendering in verse a version of the quiet and everyday difficulties of these lives, the allusiveness of the lines, and the ritualized atmosphere of the poem. These are lives that avoid tragedy, as Justice will put it in a later poem, "Simply by going on and on" ("Pantoum of the Great Depression," CP 260).

I have been discussing "Bus Stop" as if it were iambic dimeter; indeed, depending on how one scans some of the lines, at least fourteen (by a conservative count) of the poem's twenty-four lines scan strictly according to this meter. However, as Justice describes in "Bus Stop: Or, Fear and Loneliness on Portrero Hill," he was composing this poem in syllabics. As he well knew, in English a syllabic poem whose lines consist of an even number of syllables is very difficult to keep from resolving into one of the traditional accentual-syllabic meters. Ever the ready gamesman, Justice decided to try just this, writing a four-syllable line that does not fall "into the regular foot-patterns, iambs and the like, too often and too familiarly" (PS 213).

During his time in San Francisco, he was also working on "Poem to Be Read at 3 A.M.," "Memory of a Porch," "In the Greenroom," and "At a Rehearsal of 'Uncle Vanya.'" Of these the latter two are syllabic poems composed of lines of five syllables each. The syllable count of "Memory of a Porch" varies, though it seems to use a five-syllable count as a base; of its eighteen lines, half consist of five syllables. These poems are characteristic of Justice's experiments with syllabics and free verse at this time. The poems of this period also carry forward the trajectory from myth into history discernible in *The Summer Anniversaries.* Even when the poems of this later period evoke an atmosphere of ritual (as "Bus Stop" does), they are more circumstantially focused on everyday life in the world. There is, of course, no necessary reason why syllabics and free verse would be associated with a greater focus on everyday life and its struggles. It may be, though, that these experiments with new verse forms encouraged and enabled a moving away from the themes that had come to be associated with the earlier work.

The poems I discuss in this chapter appeared in Justice's second full-length collection, *Night Light,* which was published in 1967. "Poem to Be Read at 3 A.M." (CP 82), one of the two "American Sketches" in the book, is another poem about alienation, though this one features a speaker in solitude rather than one experiencing his alienation in a well-populated urban scene (as in "Bus Stop"). I take it that the title indicates the poem is to be read in a *mood* of 3 A.M., a mood of some loneliness when the world is subdued and most people are asleep. At least, such is the mood implied by the poem, in which the speaker is driving alone through a lonely place. Given this mood, the speaker finds himself feeling a kinship with the person in the "second-story room" where the light is on, if indeed there is anyone in the room at all (the poem never specifies whether the driver actually sees anyone through the window). Everything else is dark except for the diner, the only other sign of wakefulness. As to the light in the upstairs room, he can only guess that someone is there, sick or maybe reading. As projections of his own imagination, these images suggest the speaker's state of mind, some feeling of being not sick exactly, but ill at ease, accompanied by a desire to be at rest in a well-lighted place. These projections constitute the poem's main action as the speaker drives past

At seventy
Not thinking
This poem
Is for whoever
Had the light on

As "Bus Stop" suggests the possibility of seeing the urban scene as a kind of impromptu ritual in response to one's experience of alienation, "Poem to Be Read at 3 A.M." suggests establishing a passing connection by the projections of imagination. It evokes a moment of travel that both stimulates imagination and maintains its speaker on the outskirts of any scene—traveling at seventy miles per hour by car, one can scarcely be anywhere but on the outskirts.

The heightened self-consciousness of the closing lines is a hallmark of Justice's style. While any poem is composed, as the saying has it, "after the fact," not all poems so explicitly advert to this situation of the text—as this one situates itself ("This poem") as existing even though its speaker was "Not thinking" of it at the time—at least not thinking of it precisely as it turned out, for the dedication to "whoever/Had the light on" ends up as part of the poem. Curiously, the closing line even suggests that the poem somehow existed before the poet knew it. The suggestion is much in congruence with Justice's idea in "Notes of an Outsider," dated 1962–82, in *Platonic Scripts*, that "I write or try to write as if convinced that, prior to my attempt, there existed a true text, a sort of Platonic script, which I had been elected to transcribe or record" (138). J. Hillis Miller reports a similar conviction from the point of view of the reader, that a "literary work responds to or records a pre-existing perdurable alternative world" (2002, 77). The idea of the Platonic script arises in "Poem to Be Read at 3 A.M." in terms of its self-referential language, as the speaker drives by at seventy, not thinking yet who "This poem" is for. He thus speaks as if the poem already existed as he was driving by. This idea of the poem already existing creates an imaginative space where the closing lines exist both within and outside of the poem, for they both function as part of the poem and refer to the poem in retrospect. The creation of the highly self-conscious and imaginative space is one of the compensations of alienation, which allows the artistic work to occur.

There is also a curious sense in which the poem's closing speech act—a naming of what the speaker was not thinking at the time—brings the poem most fully into existence. For one thing, the closing situates the poem both in the past, at the moment of speeding by the town of Ladora, and within the moment of its composition, when the speaker finally realizes who the poem has been for all along. For another, the closing also suggests both that the text is finished before it begins and that it remains radically incomplete. A constitutive part of the poem is the failure to realize who it is for, even as the dedication is made in the closing lines. This failure is a central part of the poem, for the poem is very much about this limitation on the writer's as well as the poem's part. The incompleteness calls attention to another constitutive characteristic of any text, which is always unfinished to the extent that the reader must enter into and in effect finish it by making sense of it—reading and interpreting it. Any text must be completed in its meaning by being put into circulation and read. After the text is put into writing or print, even its author becomes another reader. These ideas are by now rather commonplace (see the essays in Tompkins), though they helpfully call attention to some of the ways that the meaning of a printed text is both here (on the page) and elsewhere (in the reader's interactions with the text), as the consciousness of any good writer and reader must be here and elsewhere also. Justice's poem calls subtle attention to these complexities that the writer and reader must negotiate.

The time at the Actor's Workshop of San Francisco allowed Justice opportunities to experiment with entering, in terms of his poems, into the fictive spaces of the theater. The writer–text–reader interactions thus became further complicated by explicit awareness of the interactions that enable theatrical text and performance to come to imaginative life. One of the plays that the company produced during Justice's tenure was Chekhov's *Uncle Vanya*, out of which came the poem "At a Rehearsal of 'Uncle Vanya'" (CP 104–5), which is tagged "San Francisco, Actor's Workshop, December 1964." The poem's persona speaks as a character in Chekhov's play, addressing the doctor, who pontificates about the wasting of the forest, as a "bit of a crank." In this the poem follows Eric Bentley's *In Search of Theater* (1953), where he refers to this character as a "crank" three times in two pages (349–50). Bentley's study is a helpful source for shedding light on Justice's sensibility, for this critic is very much aware of the extent to which the play is about life simply going on without coming to any definite or defining conclusion save for death, which is more sheer ending than conclusion. Bentley even says of Sonya's "beautiful lyric speech that ends the play" that it is "not Chekhov speaking," but rather an "overwrought girl comforting herself with an idea" (365). Further, Bentley points out the extent to which, while Chekhov remained capable of making use of "cruder forms" (366) of dramatic effect, he was also a master of nuance and subtle detail (367–68). In these latter skills, he may be considered alongside Henry James, as well as Justice himself. If Justice can be said to belong to a school of writing, then it is surely a school of nuance and subtle detail.

The poem emphasizes that the old world is indeed passing away. In this regard the doctor is not wrong. For the other characters are "burning/Your forests, doctor,/The dark green forests" in the very stove around which they huddle. By the end of the poem, the persona has adopted the first-person plural for his summary remarks:

> We hear the old nurse
> Calling her chickens
> In now: *chook chook chook.*
>
> It's cold in Russia.
> We sit here, doctor,
> In the crows' shadow.

The nurse is calling in the chickens to protect them from the crows. The poem's epigraph comes from a scene in which she expresses this concern: "The crows might get them." (Eugene K. Bristow's translation renders the line, "The crows might steal them," 61.) Having found himself in the chilling atmosphere of the play, in the shadow of these carrion birds calling attention to the death to come, the speaker registers his knowledge that life simply goes on without conclusion. One way of coping with the situation of life in this world is by entering into art, as Justice's persona has entered into the art of Chekhov's drama. Both drama and poem provide mediating structures by which to understand and negotiate the world.

In the world of theater, many deaths occur. At every performance there is a kind of death as the play ends and the characters walk offstage and are no more, replaced by the actors who play them. "In the Greenroom" (CP 103) describes the actors of the company having undergone such a death, in a space where, "Relaxing, they drop/The patronymics." But this moment outside the drama proper is not so much an escape from the artifice of the play as it is an encounter with a heightened consciousness of artificiality, where

> The sound of the axe
> Biting the wood is
> Rewound on the tape.

(This detail alludes to sound effects in Act Four of Chekhov's *The Cherry Orchard*.) As the tape is rewound in preparation for another rehearsal or performance, the actors have some time for relaxation. As the speaker queries at the end of the poem,

> What is this green for
> If not renewal?

But this green is not that of nature, any more than the sound of the axe is produced by a stagehand wielding the tool. Rather, "this green" refers to the offstage room—the greenroom of the title—where the actors go for rest and renewal, where the "old dance," and the young have not "sacrificed / Their advantages." Perhaps the most poignant lines are those that immediately follow:

> In this it is like

> A kind of heaven
> They rise to simply
> By being themselves.

But who are they here? Out of character and offstage but still in the space of the theater, their everyday identities become secondary to their dramatic roles. For within the theater, the stage character is primary. They have dropped the patronymics, though they will return to these names and the stage identities that come with them. Even the descriptions of them in this offstage space—"The cross," "The old," "The young"—suggest dramatic types. It is not that they simply become their roles, but rather that they themselves exist here precisely in relationship to their roles. Both of these poems, "At a Rehearsal of 'Uncle Vanya'" and "In the Greenroom," call attention to the interplay between life and art, the way that life derives from and depends on art as much as art derives from and depends on life. This interplay is central to Justice's work.

For Justice, "work" meant more than one thing—not only the poems, essays, and fiction that he wrote, but also the business of teaching, along with the other matters that went with being a part of the Writers' Workshop. At this time he was corresponding with Paul Engle about the possibility of taking on some administrative duties: "As for 'running the program.' As I wrote you earlier this year, I think I could handle that all right except for the fund raising."[4] Engle was legendary for his ability to raise funds to keep the workshop going and even flourishing. Understandably, Justice did not want to follow in this work. He also raised the possibility of the workshop having rotating directors, in the manner of other academic departments.

There was also, as Stephen Wilbers (109–16) explains, some trouble between the workshop and the rest of the English Department. The specific conflict, which began in 1964, is best understood against the backdrop of something that took place in the 1950s between Engle and Ray B. West, who had brought his literary magazine, the *Western Review*, to the university. The magazine was subsidized by the English Department, and Engle's attempt to draw some funds away from the review, to offer better funding to workshop students, set the stage for what occurred in the middle 1960s. On January 27, 1965, when Engle was out of town, the English Department chair made an offer to Robert Williams, a relative newcomer to the workshop, of promotion to associate professor. The move rankled several members of the workshop faculty, the most vocal of whom may have been the fiction writer Vernon Cassill, who saw the move as an attempt to shift the balance of power toward the literature faculty, as opposed to the workshop faculty, as well as to downgrade his own status by promoting a new faculty member.

Meanwhile, Gene Garber, who would step in temporarily to take over running the workshop, was visiting San Francisco. In light of the possibility that soon Engle would step down altogether from his position as workshop director, Garber solicited Justice's thoughts about how to proceed. Justice responded with a three-and-one-half-page letter to Engle dated January 28, 1965, in which he repeats his willingness to take the job, though he does not relish the prospect. He also includes an update of his own situation in San Francisco:

> There's also this. An upheaval's taking place here which has been occupying my thoughts and my time considerably the last few days. You've heard by now, I don't doubt, that the two producing directors of the company here—the Actor's Workshop—have resigned to serve as the co-directors of the Lincoln Center Repertory Theater. This apparently is going to mean that the season here will be closed down—almost immediately. I must say I feel a certain relief, feeling as I do in general about San Francisco. The company's good, as I've said before, and I think the appointment's a fine one, but I'm fairly eager to leave San Francisco, and apparently now it becomes possible, without any interruption of the Ford Grant.

In February he made a trip to Iowa City to assist with negotiations between the workshop and the English Department. Given the continuing disputes about his salary, he expressed some misgivings about returning to the workshop at all (Wilbers 115).

After these negotiations, Donald, Jean, and Nathaniel went to Florida, where they stayed with Donald's mother in Hialeah while they looked for a place to rent, which they found "in what was called South Dade, below South Miami."[5] There had been an opportunity for them to spend the summer in Massachusetts, but "Jean simply balked at the idea," which was not wholly appealing to Donald either, on "the very reasonable grounds that we'd simply been moved around too much these last couple of years, and especially this last one. We need some peace & quiet & security for a bit."[6]

The desire for some peace and security was understandable after the gloomy mood of San Francisco, but Justice also suffered a personal crisis that he could not precisely identify. Here is the opening of a letter that he wrote to Engle from Hialeah, dated February 26, 1965:

> As Mark will tell you, I suffered a kind of fugue or collapse my last day in
> Iowa City, when all the talking was done. Fatigue had something to do with
> it, & the world crisis more—but of course I don't understand it, since nothing
> quite like this had ever hit me before. Anyhow, in my present nervous state,
> I'm afraid I'd not be much help to anybody at anything. What I've prescribed
> for myself is a few months of sun & rest here near my home: it seems to be
> working pretty well in the week we've been here. We made, as you can see,
> a very quick getaway from San Francisco, with the help of Morton Marcus,
> whom you'll remember, and who happened to be around. I felt, to tell the
> truth, pretty desperate to leave & Jean agreed, with some reluctance. We
> flew—a measure of the desperation—& an agency is driving our car here.

During his time on the West Coast, Justice was preoccupied with figuring out which cities would be likely to come under attack were the Cold War tensions of the day to heat up into violence on American soil.[7] He also disliked air travel, hence the "measure of the desperation" to escape San Francisco by flying.

The next month he wrote to Engle from Miami: "I don't want to trouble you with my miseries, which are mostly in imagination anyhow but still sufficiently real to stand between me and getting anything accomplished, even so simple a thing as writing letters" (March 25, 1965). Despite the lingering difficulties, he seems to be feeling better at this point—I doubt that he would have missed the irony of writing in a letter about his inability to write letters. He nevertheless excuses himself from the "French celebration" marking the publication of *Contemporary French Poetry: Fourteen Witnesses to Man's Fate* (1965), edited by Justice and Alexander Aspel. As Engle explained in the "Postface" to this collection, Aspel (a professor of French at Iowa) selected the poems, and Justice oversaw the translations.

In May Justice wrote to Engle concerning the prospect of teaching at Iowa in the summer. He mentioned that in the past he had taught summer

courses at lower pay than the fiction writer Vance Bourjaily, an arrangement
in place because Bourjaily had to read manuscripts of novels, a "truly bur-
densome chore." But Justice also pointed out that he had had to "serve on a
good many graduate-degree committees during the summers which involve
the reading of bulky manuscripts (in some cases, novels)," and further that
"Vance himself suggested that I propose receiving some sort of compensation similar to his."[8] Justice proceeded with his summer teaching.

By the end of the summer, however, he discovered not only that the pro-
posal to increase his salary from the workshop budget had been rejected, but
also that this same budget was being tapped for a new salary line for staff.
He would ride out the regular school year, but he tendered his resignation,
effective at the end of the spring 1966 semester (Wilbers 115). In his undated
letter of resignation to John Gerber, he stated that his reasons for resigning had to do with more than salary: "So as to avoid misunderstanding, I
feel obliged to repeat that the question of money has all along been far less
important to me than questions of personal happiness and of departmen-
tal policy, especially, though not exclusively, as the operation of that policy
promises to affect the future of the workshop." He further pointed out that
if the overriding issue were money, he could have accepted an offer that
Syracuse University had made to him back in 1961, "at the rank and for the
salary at the very rate at which my pay was calculated for the teaching I did
here this summer."

Even with all of these frustrations, the 1965–66 school year was a productive one for Justice. Charles Wright, who returned to the workshop after two
years in Europe (CS 139), recalls his student days as the time that Justice
was experimenting with syllabics, working on the poems that would appear
in Night Light. Wright encountered him one night when he was headed for
the barracks that housed the workshop and asked him where he was going.
Justice replied, "I've got an idea for a poem" (ibid., 139). The poem turned out
to be "The Missing Person" (CP 89–90)—a poem written in free verse rather
than syllabics, though it fits in well with the general reorientation that his
poems were undergoing in the mid-1960s.

Justice was familiar with how a person could go missing. He had recently
edited The Collected Poems of Weldon Kees, first published in a limited edition with the Stone Wall Press (1960) and then in a trade edition with the
University of Nebraska Press (1962). In July 1955 Kees's car had been found
with the keys still in the ignition at the sightseer's lot at the Golden Gate
Bridge. His body was never recovered (Reidel 4–5, 351–52). After Justice's
"Sestina on Six Words by Weldon Kees," which uses the same end words as

Kees's "Sestina: Travel Notes," appeared in the *Hudson Review* in the spring
of 1957, the younger poet received a letter from John Kees, the missing man's
father, hoping to learn something of the possible whereabouts of his son
(Reidel 361–62). The correspondence eventually led to Justice's editing of
Kees's poems. He was later to recall Kees when writing about his own poem
"Bus Stop": "An image [that of the lights burning in unknown rooms] with
overtones of Weldon Kees, no doubt, and of the very city [San Francisco]
from which, not quite a decade before, Kees had disappeared" (PS 213).

But Justice's "Missing Person" has gone missing in a much different
sense, for he "has come to report himself/A missing person." Nor is this the
romance of the amnesiac on a quest to discover his identity in the midst of
strange and exciting circumstances, like the situation of the Gregory Peck
character in Alfred Hitchcock's *Spellbound* (see Percy 20–21); rather, he experiences himself as what is missing, as a lack or negation, or in Sartre's
terms, "like a hole in being at the heart of Being" (1956, 786). Sartre's ideas
are relevant here, for even though it is uncertain whether Justice was reading the existentialist philosopher, he certainly tried to keep up with what
was happening in the culture.[9] Existentialism—especially of the French variety, with Sartre as the preeminent public figure—had been playing a role in
American culture since the 1940s, when, as George Cotkin (92–94) points
out, it was introduced into American culture by way of the popular press
(see also Fulton 27–33 and passim). For example, Sartre published a short
article, "The Republic of Silence," as part of a series of articles titled "Paris
Alive" in the December 1944 issue of the *Atlantic Monthly*. In subsequent
years articles on existentialism, as represented especially by Sartre and Sim-
one de Beauvoir, appeared in "the pages of *Life*, the *New York Times Magazine*, *Time*, *Newsweek*, and fashion magazines such as *Vogue* and *Harper's
Bazaar*" (Cotkin 92). In a 1946 article for *Life*, Bernard Frizell set out some
of the movement's basic tenets: "Man, to an existentialist, is an individual
beset with incalculable obstacles in an unfriendly environment. What he
does with his life depends on his own stoical reaction to this environment"
(59). Rather than beginning with abstract categories, existentialist thought
seeks to begin with the sheer fact of existence. Because there is no essential
human nature, but merely a "set of potentialities permitting [humans] to
develop in a variety of directions" (62), humans are malleable, meaning that
we make ourselves, create our essences by our choices—the meaning of the
Sartrean doctrine that existence precedes essence (Sartre 1956, 565–67). By
the late 1950s, various books were published explaining existentialism to
American readers. For example, William Barrett's *Irrational Man: A Study*

in Existentialist Thought appeared in 1958, and Marjorie Grene's *Introduction to Existentialism* appeared the following year. In 1961, Hazel E. Barnes, the American translator of Sartre's *Being and Nothingness*, spoke about existentialism as part of the National Public Educational Television series "Self-Encounter" (Barnes 166–68).

As already alluded to, Sartre's doctrine of subjectivity states that human consciousness introduces nothingness into the world. As opposed to the reality of this desk or table—which is supposed to be wholly itself—the reality of human consciousness is one of distancing and detachment. As Sartre repeats throughout *Being and Nothingness*, "human reality" is a "being which is what it is not and which is not what it is" (100 and passim). Human consciousness introduces the gap between self and other, thing and thing. Thoroughly conscious of itself, human reality is always already elsewhere, beyond itself, aware of further possibilities than where it finds itself, the choices it has made, and the role it currently plays. By detaching itself from the world and even from itself, Sartrean self-consciousness begins to sound remarkably similar to Eliot's ideal of depersonalization, the distancing that makes art possible. Although Eliot and Sartre were very different thinkers—with, for example, Eliot's devotion to high-church Anglicanism and Sartre's devout atheism—they were nevertheless identifiably part of such cultural movements and networks of influence as produced the high modernist and existentialist strains of thought in the twentieth century (see Ong 1986, 22–41). Sartre, however, tended to specialize in many of the era's more anxious tendencies of thought, as in his pronouncement that "Consciousness is a being, the nature of which is to be conscious of the nothingness of its being" (1956, 86).

Such is the consciousness of "The Missing Person."[10] Wherever he drifts and whatever he does, it is himself who comes up blank, so he goes to the "authorities" with their forms, those whom he knows to "have waited/With the learned patience of barbers." The comparison to barbers is apt, for it is their job to trim away certain of the body's wilder growths, thus maintaining a look of respectability. The poem's "authorities" are the barbers of human identity. As the latter have their razors, the former have their forms, which they use to maintain the standard modes of social identity and comportment. But the Missing Person finds no comfort in them, for the blanks in the form reinforce his own blankness:

But now that these spaces in his life
Stare up at him blankly,

Waiting to be filled in,
He does not know how to begin.

Anxious that even his self-description will not coincide with himself, he seeks the reassurance of a mirror. One may be forgiven for thinking here of the Lacanian mirror stage (3-9), when the child first recognizes his or her reflected image and realizes a sense of the self as coherent and separate from others. It is not that the Missing Person is regressing to this earlier moment of development, but rather that he is seeking the reassurance of what he would have sensed about himself long ago—that he is a coherent self, that is, that his selfhood is not missing. In response to this request for reassurance, the authorities—voices of official culture encoded in laws, mores, customs, and forms—attempt to lend their own style of support:

They reassure him

That he can be nowhere
But wherever he finds himself

From moment to moment,
Which, for the moment, is here.

But their reassurance of his self-identity, that who he is coincides with his physical presence, is hardly reassuring. One line break even enforces a double entendre emphasizing what the Missing Person fears: "That he can be nowhere." He is "here," but he "can be"—could be—"nowhere," meaning both that his selfhood might not exist and that here could turn out to be nowhere after all. But even taken as a whole, these lines of reassurance limn an identity that is limited to the movement from moment to moment rather than the coherent and stable sense of self that this Missing Person presumably seeks. He exists "here," but only for the moment. The word here—one of a class of words that linguists identify as shifters—shifts radically in meaning depending on who says it where and when. Its meaning shifts the way the Missing Person's identity shifts.

Even the mirror confirms his suspicion of his own insubstantiality:
But in the mirror

He sees what its missing.
It is himself

He sees there emerging
Slowly, as from the dark

Of a furnished room
Only by darkness,

One who receives no mail
And is known to his landlady only

For keeping himself to himself,
And for whom it will be years yet

Before he can trust to the light
This last disguise, himself.

The poem fairly sparkles with double meanings—again reinforced by line breaks—though these sparks carry dark implications for this searcher. "It is himself" that he sees as missing, and while he also sees himself "there emerging," it is in a dark room that is furnished only by darkness. Such furniture provides bleak comfort. In the existence outlined here, the Missing Person maintains only minimal contact with the outside world; he receives "no mail," and the landlady knows him not by name, but rather by the reflexive pronoun whose repetition underscores his activity of "keeping himself to himself." But the crucial "as" in the lines "as from the dark / / Of a furnished room" maintains the ambiguity of this picture of a life. Is this indeed his life, or is it a simile merely illustrating how he sees himself emerging there in the mirror? I do not think that one can decide from the evidence provided by the poem alone, and I take this undecidability to reinforce further the ambiguity of this figure's identity. The closing description provides some hint of how the Missing Person sees himself—quite literally how he sees himself emerging as he gazes in the mirror. This representation of his life gives an indication of the disguise that is himself. If his disguise is himself and his very self is a disguise, then we are not far from the Sartrean idea that human reality always is what it is not and is not what it is. The disguise covers over the emptiness that this figure is. As one who is aware of his own lack, the Missing Person becomes the hero of his own existential awareness. He is left with a sense of his own nothingness. And as "The Thin Man" says in another moment of double meaning, "Nothing suffices" (CP 88). The "nothing" of human consciousness becomes the reality that will do.

By the spring of 1966, Justice was prepared to accept a new offer from the University of Syracuse. There he met the poet Philip Booth, who recalls in a brief memoir Justice's love of high-stakes poker. An anecdote illustrates how high the stakes could be: "Once early on, when he was opening his mail on the HL [Hall of Languages] steps, I remember Don's grin as he reared his head back and handed me an envelope from Alaska, with its poker check for seven hundred dollars enclosed. He exhaled something between a *Whew* and a *Whoo* and told me it came from a game five years before: 'I thought I'd never hear from that son-of-a-bitch again.' No exclamation mark, simply a wry detachment, matched with profound amusement" (CS 141–42). The amount was a handsome sum in 1966.

Such "wry detachment," considerably darkened, is one that recurs through the poems of *Night Light*, aptly titled for the subdued light of these poems, which tend to take place in atmospheres reminiscent of film noir. There are precedents for this noir style of intrigue in poetry, such as the "nameless wars and borders and betrayals of [W. H.] Auden's early poems" (Logan 2005, 66). A perusal of Auden's poems yields such moments as "He, the trained spy, had walked into the trap / For a bogus guide, seduced by the old tricks" ("The Secret Agent," 32) and "Pick a quarrel, go to war, / Leave the hero in the bar" ("Shorts," 52). Justice applies the tonalities of such intrigue to everyday life. The intrigue has to do not with anything like a spy network, but rather with something less clearly defined, something troubling to no small degree for its elusiveness. This troubling something sometimes irrupts into consciousness in the most commonplace of moments—like Sartre's Rocentin stricken with his metaphysical crisis one day as he holds up a stone at the beach (1964, 1–2). Likewise, Justice's speakers have their own understated crises in the midst of familiar, everyday circumstances.

At other times these speakers are witnesses to, if not occasions of, the crises of others, which may be crises for themselves as well. Such is the ambiguity of "The Tourist from Syracuse" (CP 98–99), a title that comes from an epigraph by the crime novelist John D. MacDonald: "One of those men who can be a car salesman or a tourist from Syracuse or a hired assassin."[11] MacDonald is perhaps best known for his novel *Cape Fear*, originally published as *The Executioners* (1957) and made into a movie in 1961 (remade in 1991). The epigraph has the hardboiled tone of Travis McGee, the protagonist of many of MacDonald's other novels. It also underscores the ambiguity of identity that one encounters in Joseph Conrad's description of Mr. Verloc, the indolent and hapless title character of *The Secret Agent*: "He might have been anything from a picture-frame maker to a locksmith" (2004, 12). One meaning of the MacDonald sentence that Justice chose as his epigraph may simply be that the man's identity is unknown, though from the looks of him he could be any of the three things named. But the sentence might also mean that the man could become all three, perhaps in quick succession. Or it could imply that he is all three at once—perhaps a car salesman touring

Syracuse while also taking care of an assignment to assassinate someone.
The epigraph emphasizes the man's potential danger. That Justice settled
on "The Tourist from Syracuse" as his title does not so much pin down the
figure's identity as it stresses displacement, for a tourist is someone on the
move, usually away from home. The sense that emerges from the poem is
that this figure's life in the world is taken up with a constant tourism of a
rather disturbing kind.

The opening lines begin to establish the speaker's ominous mode of inhabiting the world:

> You would not recognize me.
> Mine is the face which blooms in
> The dank mirrors of washrooms
> As you grope for the light switch.

It remains unclear whether the face disturbingly blooming in the dank mirror is that of the speaker himself or of the addressed "you"—the latter of
which would imply that the speaker and the "you" addressed are the same.
Is the Tourist from Syracuse hiding out in a dark washroom, or is this dark
reflection that of the speaker catching a glimpse of himself as of another,
thus setting up the divided identity of the poem? The habitual tense of these
opening lines suggests that the latter is the case, for it means that the experience is fairly commonplace, though I also suspect that the poem plays on
some possibility of both, as the reader enters into the role of the poem's addressee *groping* (the verb registers a moment of panic) "for the light switch."
Even as the poem articulates a moment of self-confrontation, it indicates the
other also lurking in the self.

The possibility that the addressed "you" (the role that the reader is asked
to play) is also the speaker haunts the whole poem, though for the time
being the speaker differentiates himself from the addressee. The disturbing
possibility is not merely that the speaker may be addressing himself, but also
that the role the reader is brought into, in negotiating the poem, turns out
to be more deeply implicated in the speaker's identity than is at first clear. In
playing the role of the addressee, the reader finds himself or herself playing
the speaker as well, and this role becomes at times only minimally human:

> My eyes have the expression
> Of the cold eyes of statues
> Watching their pigeons return
> From the feed you have scattered . . .

These eyes are not showing much life or liveliness but rather the "marble patience" of his stone-cold gaze. This figure's slow and deliberate movement associates readily with the

> shade of the awning
> Under which I stand waiting
> And with whose blackness it seems
> I am already blended.

The shade of this awning also associates the speaker with negation, the blocking out of light, the shades of his noir identity. His negating and negative voice is also that of a kind of everyman/everywoman, for when he speaks it is

> In a murmur as quiet
> As that of crowds which surround
> The victims of accidents.

The interest in victims discloses something further about the character of this speaker: his interest in the world's pain and wreckage, an interest that remains detached, for those surrounding the victims are onlookers—with something of a tourist's interest—who are neither seeking help nor engaged in providing aid.

When it comes to addressing his identity, he adverts to its fluidity as well as to his own emptiness. As he says, "My name is all names and none." He is both representative of humans and such a negation as the Missing Person finds himself to be. Like Sartre's Rocentin, he is aware of himself as "anonymous consciousness" (1964, 170). Because his very being is negation, any name will do. Congruent with this fundamental lack is his characteristic action of waiting. In Sartrean terms, one's actions, one's decisions, create what and who one is. Because existence precedes essence, the latter is formed by one's decisions, what one does with one's freedom. But one cannot avoid decision. As Sartre puts it, "I am condemned to be free" (1956, 567). Part of what this statement implies is that even a decision not to act is itself a decision; in fact, the decision "not to act" makes sense only in terms of a specific action within a given context. If, in the face of an accident, I choose "not to act," I can only do so by in fact choosing to do something else—for example, standing and watching. In choosing to wait, the Tourist from Syracuse is creating his essence; he is one who waits, who stands by while things happen. He defines himself by a lack of action, which is paradoxically its own kind of action, for it is the result of a decision.

Another meaning of Sartre's doctrine of the condemnation to freedom relevant to "The Tourist from Syracuse" relates to the dynamic of human consciousness as always already beyond what its identity has been up to the present. For human consciousness "is always something other than what can be *said* of it" (Sartre 1956, 567). Whatever my past decisions, motives, and modes of identification, whatever narrative I have constructed for my life, I am always thrown back on my freedom, which resists simple determination by what has been. Thus, the Tourist from Syracuse, having confessed that his "name is all names and none," runs through the litany of his possible modes of identity before landing on his characteristic action of waiting:

> I am the used-car salesman,
> The tourist from Syracuse,
>
> The hired assassin, waiting.

In the midst of this waiting, the speaker's address to the "you" of the poem becomes most ominous:

> I will stand here forever
> Like one who has missed his bus—
> Familiar, anonymous—
>
> On my usual corner,
> The corner at which you turn
> To approach that place where now
> You must not hope to arrive.

That single line "Familiar, anonymous"—reinforced by the off-rhyme with "bus" (a vehicle that carries people away)—encapsulates well the predicament of Sartrean self-consciousness, both familiar to itself (by being named) and anonymous even to itself (by already exceeding any narrative or name that has been attached to it). Why is it that "You must not hope to arrive" at this figure's corner? Given the implied possibility, in the opening quatrain, that the speaker and the addressee are the same, the naïve addressee must hope to avoid arriving at this moment of realization that the knowing voice of the speaker—aware of the fundamental lack and ambiguity of identity—threatens to make available. To arrive at this corner means to arrive at this place of constant waiting, where no Godot will ever arrive. To arrive at this corner means to realize that no matter how complicated one's identity, no matter how complex one's sense of self, what self one has comes to negation.

And yet this poem's intimations of emptiness, along with the Sartrean doctrines resonant with its lines, also hold out a possibility of something new. For the resistance to resigning oneself to a singularly fixed and prede-termined, fully self-present identity is a condition of freedom, which here means existing in excess of what can be said of who one is. The condition is fundamental because it is constitutive of human consciousness. It is per-ilous because it remains unpredictable, open to the possibility of the new rather than more of the same. Viewed in this way, the condition of waiting becomes less a bad-faith attempt at stasis than human awareness open to the possibility of what is to come. One must adopt a stance of waiting to the extent that what is to come cannot be predicted or fully anticipated. From this point of view, the poem's three named options of identity bear their own pointed significance. The tourist becomes the figure of human conscious-ness and identity in motion, resisting stasis. The salesman becomes the fig-ure bent on putting over a prepackaged identity. Actually, this second figure works doubly. First, that Justice turns MacDonald's "car salesman" into a "used-car salesman" emphasizes this option as among the most recogniz-able of American stereotypes or prepackaged identities—the shyster bent on unloading a bill of goods, at least as guilty of bad-faith posturing as Sartre's waiter (1956, 101–3). Second, this salesman's bill of goods is a figure of the prepackaged identity that would allow one to believe that freedom is a mi-rage. Using a prepackaged identity in an attempt to avoid the perils of free-dom is the very definition of Sartrean bad faith. The assassin then becomes the figure of human consciousness resisting its loss of freedom in a handily scripted identity—for example, the philosopher, the scholar, the poet—that one might authentically use, though which becomes bad faith when used as an always-already, self-evident, self-present given by which to avoid one's perilous freedom. The latter figure assassinates the ready-made and too-convenient patterns. That the poem retains its ominous tone registers its recognition of the possible dangers and dangerous turns of resistance to the ready-made.

I have thus far related the themes of the ambiguity and tenuousness of identity in Justice's poems at this time to the infusion of French existential-ism into American culture. Another important influence, read and discussed among his friends, is a work of history, Jean Overton Fuller's *Double Webs: Light on the Secret Agents' War in France* (1958).[12] This book had such an ef-fect that Justice's friend Richard Stern wrote a novel based on it (*In Any Case*, 1962; reprinted as *The Chaleur Network* in 1982), and it inspired in Justice's friend and Iowa classmate Henri Coulette a sequence of poems, "The War of the Secret Agents" (1966). Although Fuller's book did not inspire a similarly direct treatment in any of Justice's writing, a consideration of her study will help to illuminate some of Justice's emphases.

The book considers double agents during World War I, specifically what happened in relation to the "Prosper Network," part of the French Section of Britain's Special Operations Executive (the SOE), whose principal work in the war effort against the Central Powers was the "equipment and organization of a secret army" (13). The Prosper Network had been betrayed by a double agent, and at the time that Fuller came onto the scene to research her book, much of the blame had fallen on Major Gilbert Norman, code named "Archambault," second in command under the agent code-named "Prosper." But Gilbert Norman could never be interviewed about his actions during the war years, for he had died in a Nazi concentration camp (98). The dead man's father expended considerable energy trying to clear his son's name.

There was a basic confusion over the identity of the betrayer that centered on a name, for another, earlier suspect had been the agent in the Prosper Network code-named "Gilbert."[13] Although charges were brought against "Gilbert" in the matter of the betrayal of the network, he was cleared; nevertheless, some continued to believe in his guilt. When Fuller interviewed "Gilbert" (184–223), he maintained his innocence after a fashion, though he also hinted that the story as it occurred on the ground was more complex than any version that had thus far appeared in print. The basic theories circulating at the time held that some British operatives posing as double agents became actual double agents working with the German forces. The language of this version quickly becomes quite complicated—for it is increasingly difficult to track who is who and for what purposes they are acting—and it is precisely such complication and even more that "Gilbert" maintained to be the case. As he put it: "Spying is not a business for angels. It is only to people who do not understand this that some of the shifts to which I refer would look black" (195–96). Fuller then picks up with her own further commentary: "He wanted to say that some of the people whose names occurred in my books had put their foot in it in one way or another, but he did not mean, by saying that, to blacken them" (196).

By the time she comes to her closing reflections, Fuller finds herself in some agreement with "Gilbert," to the extent that the actual story on the ground must surely have been more complex than she had previously thought; however, she remains uncertain about the precise details. She comes to suspect, though, that something had gone terribly wrong in London—misjudgments, poor planning, etc. Part of the problem might have been that the SOE was a relatively amateur organization, staffed by people with very little experience in secret work before the war. Gilbert Norman, for example, had worked as an apprentice in a firm of chartered accountants. By contrast, "Gilbert" had already been involved in secret work. Fuller provides a summary account of what she learned:

> The concept of the double-agent is well enough known to readers of the literature of espionage; it is understood well enough that the authorized double-agent may be instructed or licensed by his own side to contact the enemy and play in semblance the part of a traitor, in order to gain knowledge of the enemy's work such as he could scarcely obtain unless he became part of the enemy's working machine; but is it so often asked what price he has to pay? For the enemy whose workings he penetrates in this way will certainly require something from him. The object is, of course, to gain more for his own side than he is obliged to give away to the other; one writer on these subjects has likened the process to the children's game of "swops," but in "swops" as in any other contest one risks being the loser. The authorized double-agent who pays in good faith too dearly is not, therefore, a traitor, though of course such a double-agent may always turn real traitor, and the dividing line might be hard to draw. (230)

As the literature of espionage has disclosed (see Hepburn 3–13), when one plays such games of intrigue, the role that one adopts can become who one is; for the image of the spy—especially the double agent—emphasizes the fluidity of identity and affiliation. When the role has to do precisely with playing at dual identities, the ambiguities of selfhood become quite complicated. Joseph Conrad articulates something of the issue in *Under Western Eyes* (1911), when he describes Razumov, who has been mistakenly taken into the confidence of a revolutionary cabal: "He felt, bizarre as it may seem, as though another self, an independent sharer of his mind, had been able to view his whole person very distinctly indeed" (169). But what happens when this "independent sharer" no longer sees the "whole person very distinctly" at all? What happens when these two intermingle and become confused? We do well to read such poems as "The Missing Person" and "The Tourist from Syracuse" in relation to conditions of deeply ambiguous identity, thus bringing the intrigue of the double agent into the realm of everyday life. These figures find themselves in a confusing and foreign realm, a realm that is themselves.

As mentioned above, Fuller's book proved compelling to Justice and many of his friends. In Richard Stern's fictional version of the story, the father of the dead spy named Robert Curry (Stern's version of Gilbert Norman), seeking to clear his son's name, plays the investigative role that Fuller herself plays in her nonfiction account. Stern's novel thus also explores the shifts of identity from one generation to another. As Robert Curry's father, Samuel, says at one point: "Young men since the war are beyond me. They're remarkably purposive, but the purpose is secretive or even disguised. It's as if they were all members of undergrounds" (165). The idea of the underground, as of espionage generally, with its complexities of identity, is transferred to negotiations of everyday life. Although the identity most explicitly in question in the novel is that of Robert Curry, the narrative comes to concern itself just as much with the identity of his father. Released from his everyday preoccupations with his successful business, Samuel, in setting out to clear his son's name, also sets out to investigate who he is himself, raising the question of whether his own identity is any more real than that of a double agent. As one critic has said of the novel, "While the fact that [*In Any Case*] was reprinted with the title *The Chaleur Network* indicates that it has maintained continued appeal in the spy genre, the intrigue does not really come from this aspect of the novel but from the other forms of guilt, betrayal and redemption that the espionage context provides an excuse for portraying" (Izzo 80–81). These forms of guilt, betrayal, and redemption become part of the everyday intrigue.

In his 1944 essay for the *Atlantic Monthly* "The Republic of Silence," Sartre writes of fighting as a member of the French resistance in terms that could apply outside the context of war: "To those who led clandestine lives, the conditions of their fight brought a new experience. They did not fight in the daylight, like soldiers; in every circumstance they were alone; they were pursued and arrested in their solitude." Fuller reflects on the struggles that humans generally face in circumstances of solitude. At the end of her chapter "Reflections," she includes "four lines of doggerel verse" that she says kept running through her mind as she was working on the chapter:

> There is so much good in the worst of us,
> And so much bad in the best of us,
> That it ill behooves any one of us
> To judge another of us. (237)

She goes on to write, "If the second line is salutary to remember, to the first I can bear witness. It is the lasting thought that I should like to leave with the reader. For therein lies the capacity of the human heart to gain the day" (237).

Another work that uses the device of an assumed identity to explore the possibilities of the "capacity of the human heart to gain the day" is *The*

Hound of Earth (1955), by Justice's colleague at the Writers' Workshop Vance Bourjaily. In this novel, Allerd Pennington, a military scientist who has helped to build the atomic bomb, goes AWOL "on the same day that the explosion of the first atomic bomb at Hiroshima was announced" (11). Even though Pennington was not aware that his work was going toward the building of this horrific weapon, he cannot live with himself knowing what his work has led to. He therefore tries to flee who he was when he was engaged in this work. As he writes to his wife after his disappearance, "Can you think of me as a living suicide, spared the inelegant fuss of real dying, and of this as the final note?" (12–13). He has committed "suicide," or tried to do so, in the sense of fleeing the world within which his older identity came to be. He lives from job to job, making enough money to get by and then moving on before he gets established in a new life long enough for the authorities to find him.

But he can never really escape himself. It is not only that he carries his memories with him, but also that he constantly encounters himself in interaction with others, and these interactions always bring him back to himself, not as a static entity, but rather as a being who realizes himself because of his connections to and relationships with others. Selfhood emerges in relationship to others. Sartre gets at something of this dynamic when he writes, "I need the Other in order to realize fully all the structures of my being" (1956, 303). Insofar as Sartre emphasizes conflict as the fundamental mode of relationship between self and other (see 1956, 477, 555, and passim), he gets at only a part of the story that Bourjaily's novel tells. On the one hand, Pennington acts in conflict with the community of effort that produced the atomic bomb, as well as in conflict with the version of himself that lived and worked as a part of that community. On the other hand, he finally cannot avoid involvement with the others he encounters in his exile from his old life. Even though he has tried to diminish his selfhood by minimizing his human contacts and interactions, he finds himself unable to avoid entanglement with the needy lives of the people he works with at his job in the toy section of a department store during the Christmas season. The cost of this entanglement is allowing himself to be sufficiently settled in the world to enable the government authorities to track him down. It is this involvement in the lives of others that the narrator associates with Pennington's humanity:

> And so he was caught at last. He had tried to run and, weary of running, rested; and resting, been unable to reject forever and ended by accepting them all: his love for Nickie, his pity for Finn, his responsibility to Tom, his fascination

and compassion for the horror of Dolly, the impulse to oppose M'nerney—the need to take his stand. These things had held him, involved him, chased and trapped him, deprived him of his freedom to live alone with guilt—the hound of earth had caught him. No man, no matter what his time, his country, his condition, training, heredity or philosophy, forever escapes that hound, his own humanity. (249–50)

In the face of the horror that he has unwittingly cooperated in building, Pennington seeks to alienate himself from the human lifeworld, to float along its edges. Ironically, it is because of his sense of ethical responsibility, with its implications of connectedness to others, that he seeks this existence of alienation. It is then this very ethical sense that leads him to reenter more fully the world that he never really escaped. The convictions that led to his flight are also those that lead to his involvement.

Henri Coulette, in "The War of the Secret Agents," took up Fuller's book in explicit terms. The theme of double identity arises in the following lines spoken by Kieffer, the German contact of the double agents in the SOE:

> I begin to know Prosper and his comrades.
> There are even times
> when I can sense their terror;
> it is as though I were watching, too,
> gazing up at my own office, at this light,
> myself gazing at myself. (1966, 62)

But here taking on more than one identity ironically leads to a loss of self. As illustrated in lines spoken by the agent named "Cinema," it is as if by coming together, these various identities cancel each other out, leaving one a blank:

> I was a courier
> and rode the Métro, disguised differently
> everyday. I was no one,
>
> I was what I seemed, I did not have to think.

If one can change appearances at will, and one is what one seems, then identity—along with the self disclosed by identity—quickly becomes an emptiness. In the literature of espionage, the paradigmatic case of this utter loss may be Robert Ludlum's Jacob Bourne of *The Bourne Identity* (1980), who can remember neither his everyday nor his assumed identity. Although he retains some of the skills and knowledge of his former life as a spy, he remains adrift in the world until he is able to recover parts of that former self. While self and identity may not be precisely the same, one tends to inform the other, and a loss of identity—in much of the writing discussed here—amounts to some loss of self, even as such loss can also open one to the possibility of creating a new identity and a new or renewed sense of self. The latter is much the case with Bourjaily's Allerd Pennington.

In his poem "The Unbroken Code," another of Justice's friends (and another Iowa classmate), Robert Dana, responds to Coulette's "The War of the Secret Agents." The poem, from Dana's *The Power of the Visible* (1971) begins,

Agent of obscure
powers, countries whose names, whose
locations even, he

cannot now recall. (1991, 36–37)

"The Unbroken Code" works as a shrewd summary of the situation of the double agent in everyday life, living (or trying to live) even after his or her place has been forgotten, leaving the agent to wander through the world—like those men who will "wander aimlessly through cities" in Justice's "Young Girls Growing Up (1911)" (*The Sunset Maker*, 1987). Further, the agent in Dana's poem

cannot distinguish,
some days, his real

from his coded name.

He thus submits to the confusion of identity on which much of the literature surveyed here dwells.

I have taken the time for this survey not only to create a picture of the milieu that Justice was working in, but also to call attention to specific themes and preoccupations informing Justice's poetry at this time. These include the implied metaphor of the double agent in everyday life; the loss of identity, along with the concomitant loss of a sense of self; becoming what one plays at; and the possibility that a loss of identity can, at times, lead to a deepening of self, a transformation of who one is. The double agent in everyday life may wander aimlessly because of the very loss of identity that can open him or her to a transformative deepening of self and renewal of identity. While this perspective may help to make sense of many of Justice's poems, it is especially helpful with regard to "The Missing Person."

At the beginning of the poem, we encounter the Missing Person already in a state of displacement. His gesture of reporting himself to the authorities as missing indicates some desire to regain a sense of self by a connection to other humans; he is notifying the authorities whose job includes drawing the missing back into a human community. However, once he sees that to make these human connections he must conform to the expectations of the form that he has been handed, he draws back from the possibility. Rather than fill in the blanks—that is, rather than embrace the points of identification that he would have to accept were he to fill out the form—he chooses to continue as the Missing Person, who must remain blank. In resisting the clear identification that he at first pursued by reporting to the authorities, he refuses the role that he would be expected to play in the world, along with the reassurance of his identity and place. As Mark Strand wrote with regard to this poem, "Just as the past exercises its peculiar strength by having become past, so the self can be more compelling, paradoxically present when lost" (580). Even though the Missing Person "might like to believe them"— to believe, that is, the authorities and their reassurances—he must remain the Missing Person, resisting the homogenization of the official forms. A paradox remains in play with this identification, for while the title "The Missing Person" affords our anti-hero a kind of identity, this identity is one of nonidentity, that of one who occupies the role of a lack, a space, one who is always elsewhere, displaced.

The vision of this person's life that emerges in the latter part of the poem remains uncertain. The image of home that the poem provides remains merely a possibility, for he sees himself emerging "*as* from the dark / Of a furnished room" (emphasis mine). What his literal life might be remains unclear. As Justice's speaker says in the title poem of *The Sunset Maker*, "*As if*... but everything there is is that" (CP 235, emphasis in original). In other words, the literal sense of the life, as of the person—if "literal" is to mean self-identical, univocal, monological—is not available at all, for the person and the life can be spoken of only by means of displacement, the mode of "as if." If the Missing Person seeks reassurance of the coherence of his place and identity in the imagery that he sees in the mirror, the poem displaces this coherence back into the play of difference and differentiation.

Nevertheless, this imagery of the poem's latter half provides at least a fantasy of human contact, a vision of a life in which he is "known to the landlady," even if only as one who keeps "himself to himself." It is a vision admitting the necessity of some sort of encounter with other people in a human world. At the same time, the "as if" gesture provides a lightness of touch to the description that prevents the poem, along with the Missing

Person, from falling into a vision of singular and self-identical life. This human consciousness is always somehow beyond the immediate scene, always
already elsewhere. Viewed from this perspective, the condition of being a
missing person means resisting a mode of life that pretends to be summed
up and made fully adequate and explicit in terms of a given role, a mode that
Sartre identifies as "bad faith" (see 1956, 86–116). Being a missing person
means maintaining the precarious dynamism of human freedom. Even if
the Missing Person would like to take comfort in the security of the official
forms, he finally resists.

The poem's crucial turn occurs at line twenty-two, signaled by the coordi-
nate conjunction "but":

And he might like to believe them.
But in the mirror. . . .

This turn marks the moment where the speaker is pulled away from the
authorities' reassurances and into the ambiguous vision of the mirror, where
he sees emerging an emblem of his life, ending with "This last disguise, himself." The line is deceptively simple but becomes increasingly complicated
when pressed for implication. The two terms—"disguise" and "self"—stand
as separate, but if "himself" is read as an appositive, then this "last disguise"
is "himself." Or the line could mean that the self is its own unique *kind* of
disguise, the *last* disguise, unlike any other. One could also read the line
as implying that the self is merely another disguise like others, privileged
by nothing more than circumstance and historical accident—no different in
kind from other disguises. The line could even imply that one becomes a self
by playing at one's disguise, which in turns becomes who one is, though not
all of who one is; for if my disguise becomes who I am, then the self that I
become is as subject to change as my previous self.

I take it that the two major terms of the closing line—"disguise" and
"self"—remain in dialectical tension. However deeply the two are related,
they are sufficiently different to keep pulling apart, only to associate once
again in a new way. According to the Oxford English Dictionary, the word
disguise bears the root sense of "to put out of one's usual guise, manner, or
mode," and the word *self* bears the root sense of "same." Thus, whereas the
disguise is as changeable as a suit of clothes, as subject to revision as one's
performance, the self is what remains the same. However, given the association between the two terms in Justice's poem, their senses intertwine. The
disguise is not merely ephemeral, for it has bearing on the formation of the
self. At the same time, the self never remains the same, for it is constantly

modified by the guises that it wears. There is, as Gerard Manley Hopkins wrote, a "taste of myself . . . more distinctive than the taste of ale or alum" (quoted in Ong 1986, 28), but this is a self more process than product, more motion than monument. It is self-reflexive and developmental, trying out new identities as it proceeds to work with itself. Because it is never the self-same, sunk into a singular identity, it also experiences itself as displaced, in some ways lost. In the terms developed here, we may also come to a provisional distinction between self and identity. The former is how an embodied consciousness experiences itself from within, whereas the latter is the presentation of this self to the world. It is important to bear in mind, however, that this distinction cannot hold in absolute terms, for self-consciousness requires interaction with others, meaning that one's outward presentation is constantly a part of one's sense of self, just as one's sense of self also informs one's self-presentation, the interactions of which modify one's sense of self, etc.—the process is constant. To be a self in this dynamic sense means also to be a missing person, for this vision of personhood means that the self can never be static and purely locatable, but is rather constantly on the move.

Of *Night Light*'s poems of displaced selves, "The Man Closing Up" (CP 91–93) may be the least yielding to clear sense. Tagged "improvisations on themes from Guillevic" (one of the poets included in the anthology that Justice edited with Alexander Aspel, but not one whom Justice translated), the poem speaks of the life of a representative figure, whose designation—like that of "The Missing Person"—functions partly as a name and partly as a disclosure of his mode of being in the world. Ironically for a figure closing up, his characteristics at first open toward the outer world of the landscape:

Old pilings, rotted, broken like teeth,
Where a pier was,

A mouth,
And the tide coming in.

The man closing up
Is like this.

Here the man's life simply goes on like the movements of the tide. There is no purpose other than what the Man Closing Up might choose to pursue. As in many of Justice's poems, there are remnants of a past world—the remains of a pier—leaving the present a diminished version of what once was. The Man Closing Up partakes of this diminished life. Ironically, this figure longs for a Platonic kind of purity. But the poem illustrates that to survive and to act, one must swerve away from a pursuit of this Platonic realm of the absolute into a life engaged in the material world. What purity one accomplishes must be in terms of the ambiguities and muddiness of the material realm.

But to evade materiality, this figure passively feeds on diminishment, as the "mouth" of section one feeds on the tide, preparing for the focus on hunger in section two—or rather, the focus on the lack of hunger, for he "has no hunger / For anything." Here he becomes an echo of Kafka's "Hunger Artist" living in alienation from the human world because he finds himself uninterested in the pleasures that others take for granted. The alienation of Justice's artist of closure at first seems even more severe, for even though Kafka's Hunger Artist has no desire for food, the story nevertheless suggests some desire for recognition from the public. Justice's Man Closing Up does not hunger for anything at all, not even the "rich refusals" of "The Thin Man" (CP 88). Ironically, however, as the poem proceeds, the man's very refusals lead to multiple desires, which remain inescapable.

For example, section three hints that he might desire something after all: sleep, perhaps oblivion. But even here the language withholds direct statement of desire:

He would make his bed,
If he could sleep on it.

The conditional statement points in the direction of what he would do, but not necessarily what he wants. Even though there is some slight reassurance that something like a human desire could infiltrate this rather alien being's experience—for choice suggests a movement toward something, a motion very like desire—the withholding of direct statement ensures that he remains relatively blank. The language is oblique, for the Man Closing Up can be approached only by indirection.

This ultimate ascetic exists only for the language that sustains him. Observed as a man made out of words (to adapt Stevens's phrasing), the white sheets that he would use to make his bed become the white sheets of blank pages. The blankness of these sheets and the possibility that the man would "disappear into the white" reveal a devotion to the empty page, calling to mind Justice's idea of the "Platonic script" that he describes in "Notes of an Outsider" (quoted earlier), the idea that he writes as if "prior to my attempt, there existed a true text, a sort of Platonic script, which I had been elected to transcribe or record" (PS 138). If the material text is one that always swerves, as it must, away from the uninscribed ideal—for in the Platonic dispensation, the material copy always in some way violates the essential idea—then the greatest poem is one that remains unwritten. Only in this way can it exist in the realm of the ideal.

The ideal material poem, then, is one that calls attention to its own imperfection in such a way as to displace the reader's attention onto the ideal. "The Man Closing Up" functions in this way by means of the poem's fragmentary language and disjunctive narrative, hinting that it is, like the remnants of the pier in section one, composed of what remains from the past. As a denizen of this material text, the Man Closing Up can hope only for oblivion, for he would

> disappear into the white,
>
> Like a man diving,
> If he could be certain
>
> That the light
> Would not keep him awake,
>
> The light that reaches
> To the bottom.

Here is where the poem comes closest to affirming the closing-up-man's desire, a longing for the purest oblivion in sleep, perhaps the sleep of death. Like Hamlet, though, he does not know "what dreams may come" (3.1.66) to disturb his rest.[14] What is this light that threatens to keep him awake, the light that "reaches / To the bottom"? The light that reaches to the bottom of consciousness? to the bottom of actuality? I take it to be anything of this material world, including the world of the text, that might disturb his vision of purity. In the old dispensations of Platonic and neo-Platonic thought (such as in Plotinus), light functions as the primary metaphor of ultimate reality. But in his desire for purity, the Man Closing Up will not settle for anything involving metaphor, not even the ultimate metaphor of ultimate reality, for metaphor brings one back to the rustle of things in the world. In the classic modes of thought just referred to, light represents not only ultimate reality, but any reality, which reflects something of the ultimate light. In his desire for purity (the purity of oblivion, the purity of the blank page—ironically, his desires proliferate as the text proceeds), the Man Closing Up will not accept any light at all. In a longing for absolute purity, oblivion becomes the alternative to accepting even the imperfection of material light. Because he cannot get to the pure Platonic ideal, he longs for nothingness instead, the only kind of purity he might credibly attain. As with "The Thin Man," his is the purity of negation.

In the fourth and fifth sections, the poem's light becomes the literal light of a lighthouse, even if it exists only in the closing-up-man's head. His consciousness cannot escape the materiality that his longing for purity would negate. If I am correct in my reading of this figure, then he would surely have preferred that the poem end with section three—or that the pages remain blank, or even that there were no pages at all. But here is why the poem needs the third-person narrator, and why the Man Closing Up does not speak: his is an aesthetic of pure withholding. He therefore needs a narrator, who brings the details of the literal light and the literal lighthouse into the poem.

Section four finds the Man Closing Up in his most characteristic action: closing the windows and trying the doors—emblems of his desire to close out the details of the world. But he cannot close out the shiftings of the ambiguous world of himself, as becomes especially evident in the fifth section, where the pronoun "it" shifts in meaning until it becomes a staircase that runs up and down the side of a lighthouse inside the man's head. But he is not, as it turns out, the keeper of the lighthouse, as section four would seem to suggest. Rather, the keeper, who clangorously ascends "Rung after rung," exists in the lighthouse in the head of the Man Closing Up. It is this man within the Man Closing Up who most explicitly desires something:

> He wants to keep the light going,
> If he can.

Again, as a thoroughly literal and material light, this figure of the lighthouse light belongs to the materiality of the world and the text.

In this fifth and final section, a rather oblique conflict emerges between the Man Closing Up and the lighthouse keeper within. As the poem states, the word that "goes around" is

> a staircase,

> An iron staircase
> On the side of a lighthouse.
> All in his head.

> And it makes no sound at all
> In his head,
> Unless he says it.

This staircase that remains quiet unless he says the word is the one that the keeper clangorously ascends. But the Man Closing Up opts for silence; as the poem concludes, "the man closing up / Does not say the word." Whereas the Man Closing Up wants to escape the light and refuses to say the word, the keeper opts for noise and wants to keep the light going. Because the poem has continued beyond the closing-up-man's longing for oblivion and silence, the voice of the narrator is on the side of the lighthouse keeper who remains engaged in the material world, engaged in language and the text; this keeper trusts himself to the artificial light that provides illumination even if imperfectly (like that light in the upstairs window in "Poem to Be Read at 3 A.M."). Although the closing-up-man's labors and longings oppose those of the lighthouse keeper, the latter remains a part of the former. The keeper maintains the very artificial light in relationship to which the Man Closing Up can long for the negation of the world's light. Without a relationship to the material world, one cannot articulate a longing for purity, for such articulation depends on the constant displacement of materiality, including the materiality of words.

Although the Man Closing Up does not speak, the eros and movement of language continue in motion in the poem, for the telling of this tale of refusal and restraint exists as a poem. It is a description of this secret life that can be told only in terms of a falling away from the hidden life that the poem discloses. The closing-up-man's refusal to speak unleashes the eloquent if fragmentary speaking of the poet who tells his tale. In one sense, the ideal figure remains the unspeaking man who exists outside of the compromises of his desire for purity, but his is an ideal available only within the eros of language's constant movement. As in the other poems that I have been considering in this chapter, "The Man Closing Up" demonstrates that identity, however ephemeral it may be, is what one achieves in confronting one's lack of identity. This achievement is mediated to no small degree by the displacements effected by language.

In a chapter about the poems of *Night Light*, I would be remiss were I not to consider "Men at Forty" (CP 86), one of Justice's more widely anthologized poems. Like the other poems discussed so far, this one is about loss—represented by the "doors to rooms" that men at forty "will not be / Coming back to"—and the concomitant shifts of identity, though the themes are treated here more subtly. The figures of the title experience the movement of their lives simply by standing in one place:

At rest on a stair landing,
They feel it moving
Beneath them now like the deck of a ship.

The lives that they are living carry them along like a ship taking them they-don't-know-where, even though they experience their lives also as embedded in one place. Taking a cue from the "mortgaged houses" of the final line, we may take the mortgages, with all of the debt and obligations implied, as representative of why these men's lives move along like the deck of a ship, beyond their control—they cannot escape their debts and obligations. As with the "lives we lead / But do not own" of "Bus Stop," their lives are living them as much as they are living their lives.

Even as they remain anchored by their mortgages, their identities are in flux. If they encounter in mirrors the "face of the boy as he practices tying / His father's tie," they also see their own roles shifting to those of the older generation, for "They are more fathers than sons themselves now." The sound in the final quatrain "Of the crickets, immense, / Filling the woods" underscores this emphasis on flux, for because sound "exists only when it is going out of existence" (Ong 1982, 32), it calls attention to ephemerality as no other sense does, even though all sensation occurs in time. Further, this sound of the crickets' stridulation is a "twilight sound," calling attention to the coming of night as well as the coming twilight of these figures' lives. That this passing sound occurs in the precincts of the mortgaged houses calls attention to a combination of stability and ephemerality, over neither of which these men at forty have much of anything like control. They must stay where they are, paying off the mortgage while their lives carry them along.

In the spring of 1967, Justice received a fellowship from the National Endowment for the Arts that allowed him to take the fall term off. During this time he delivered the Elliston Lectures at the University of Cincinnati. Philip Booth recalled Justice's anxious preparations and read drafts of three of the lectures; the remaining three Justice would have to compose while living in Cincinnati. Another artist at Cincinnati was John Cage, who had become composer-in-residence in 1967. Justice recognized the distinction of this experimental writer and composer, but he remained suspicious. "You know," Booth recalled him saying in confidential tones, "he's the enemy" (CS 145).

But as it turned out, Justice and Cage got along very well. They were part of a high-stakes poker game after which Justice gave Cage a ride home.[1] That evening Justice had won two hundred dollars. The composer-in-residence told him that up to that point, the highest stakes he had ever played for ran to several quarters. Cage was one of the poets on whom Justice lectured while at Cincinnati; he asked Cage not to attend the lecture on his own work, and Cage obliged.

Even if he were in some sense "the enemy," Cage won Justice over. He is of course well known for his experiments with chance operations, associated with several modes of the avant-garde, especially surrealism (see Bürger 64–68, and Nadeau 49–50, 56–58). According to David Revill, Cage had begun using aleatory methods in his musical compositions in the early 1950s and then later took them up in his composition of poems also (131, 136). At least once he even used chance methods in putting together a lecture (199). He would throw the I Ching, flip coins, or shuffle cards as ways of taking advantage of chance (149). Over the years he continued to refine his methods, for it can be surprisingly difficult to allow chance free play. Sometimes he set up situations "so that chance generates the conditions in which choice must be exercised" (135). Cage was, of course, well aware of the difficulties: "The avoidance of intention through chance operations depends paradoxically on intentionally setting up the parameters within which chance will operate"

(156). Later in his life, he even used chance operations in painting (285). Justice seems to have been influenced by his contact with Cage. Booth notes that upon his return to Syracuse from Cincinnati, Justice demonstrated the aleatory methods he was using to write poems (CS 145–46).

In a 1975 interview, Justice described how he conducted his experiments:

> I wrote down on note cards a lot of words from poems I liked. I chose a good number of sentences which interested me as sentences, as syntactical forms, and I wrote these down on another set of note cards. I divided the word cards up into three groups, nouns, verbs, and adjectives, from which I thought I could generate any other parts of speech necessary to deal with the sentences. I then shuffled the sentence cards, as I called them, and dealt myself a sentence, you might say, and where the sentence called for a noun, I shuffled the noun cards and dealt myself a noun. And where it called for a verb, the same. And so on. I found in working around with this that chance wasn't all that good to me the first time through, so on some large sheets of paper I tried filling in each sentence three times. Then I would have what seemed a multitude of choices, but actually a workable limit, and having three words to choose from in each place in each sentence meant that I could generate a number of sentences from each sentence card, and I could go on for as many sentences as I wanted to. By then I might have quite a few lines and I found that when things were going well, when I was being dealt winning hands, so to speak, the sentences seemed to cohere to some degree; and where they cohered to a lesser degree than I approved of, I was willing to violate chance and impose myself, to make connections or to leave things out. (PS 55–56)

Like Cage, Justice saw his experiments as an interplay between chance and choice. Some of the poems that he generated by this method would later appear in his third full-length volume of poems, the aptly titled *Departures* (1973), in which he most radically departed from what he had previously written.

In the meantime *Night Light* appeared. In general the reviews echo those of *The Summer Anniversaries* in their emphasis on the author's skill and the overt literariness of the poems. W. H. Pritchard, in his brief treatment of the book in a Poetry Chronicle for the *Hudson Review* (summer 1967), faults many of the poems for being "about literature, often not very exciting literature" (CS 227). Writing for the *Denver Quarterly* (summer 1967), Robert Pawlowski reminds his readers that as a form of art, poetry "must concern itself with the precision of its forms and instruments and with the feelings and insights of its writers. These concerns demand ultimately that the artist exercise a ruthlessly responsible and self-conscious command of them" (ibid., 224). If the artist attends to these difficult matters of technique, as Justice does, theme and vision will follow, for the poet is after all a human being as well as an artist.

In his review for *Poetry* (July 1968), William Hunt takes his measure of the distance between the poems' ambitions and what they believe to be possible. It is not that Justice fails as a poet, but rather that as an artist he confronts the limitations of what art can accomplish. Hunt connects this sensibility to a worldview and a sense of history: "The poems in *Night Light* labor under the apprehension that once upon a time there was a possibility to get it all down on paper, for all time in one poem, but no longer" (CS 234–35). This myth of the fully adequate text, like that of the "Platonic script," is one that Justice used as a creative device; he did not fully believe this view of history, that there was a time when all could be gotten "down on paper"—he may not have believed it at all—but he found it a compelling vision for his life as an artist.

This provisional idea of the world and of history echoes what I set out in chapter 2 concerning Justice's vision of the sublime, which one can experience only in passing, in a moment of realizing that it is lost. The poems of *Night Light*, as well as those that he was working on to be included in *Departures*, disclose a knowledge of the losses that have always already occurred in the world of human experience, including the losses that are a part of language. The gods and heroes of the old poems no longer walk the earth; they no longer inhabit our poetry as they once did, nor can they. In the postmodern era, the only way credibly to include the old gods and heroes is through irony and other distancing techniques that deliver a glance of these ancient figures before they once more disappear beyond the horizon.

According to this mythic vision of history, the perfect poem can no longer be uttered, but one can nevertheless catch a passing glimpse of the poet hero who once uttered the perfection of art. This heroic figure is Orpheus, whose words had power and immediate effects in the world. His "lyre carries the music of universal harmony and eternal response" (Hassan 5). In his later work, Justice will turn his attention more and more to this figure, though the vision of this mythic artist also has relevance to the poems of this, the middle period of Justice's work, where the focus is on a state of fallenness from a fully adequate past. But even the ancient tales we have of Orpheus are stories of loss intimated in a language conceived as diminished and inadequate. We never really hear Orpheus sing, any more than we hear the Sirens whose sublime music casts Odysseus into exquisitely painful throes of ecstasy. The days of gods and heroes are always past tense. Even Homer sings of days long past. And within the *Iliad*, the aged Nestor speaks of how the great days of the Trojan War are diminished in comparison with what he can recall, the days when men fought centaurs and "wild things of the mountains." As he says of these early warriors, "Men like those/I have not seen again, nor shall" (bk. 1). The world of greatest grandeur—of gods, heroes, and great deeds—is always the world that is lost.

I suspect that there are deep psychological dynamics, related to the uncertainties of worldly experience, at play in this vision (see Eliade 49–130). The myth of an ideal past enables a fantasy of something that one might get back to, or at least glimpse in passing. It is a fantasy that Justice's work indulges in only with great self-consciousness, as befits the postmodern situation, where the utter loss of the gods and heroes who never actually existed is embraced as never before. The poet can no longer credibly tell the old tales, though she or he can speak of diminished circumstances in a language wholly embraced as inadequate, and there is an uncanny grandeur in such a stance. It is as if, in denying the possibility of grandeur, a hint of the sublime emerges, like a vision one can glimpse only after looking away. What is left of the grand illuminations of the mythic past are the night lights allowing brief insights into the passing lives of the present world.

In the Justices' lives, the turbulence of the present world was much in evidence, as in the student unrest on many of the country's university campuses. Jean Justice writes that there was in Syracuse "a kind of riot in our neighborhood, not bad, but a gang of people roamed through our nearest shopping street one morning, breaking windows, etc."[2] Donald wanted to leave Syracuse because he found the new department chair, as well as the town, in some ways disagreeable.

In the fall of 1970, he was a visiting professor at the University of California at Irvine, and the fall of 1971 saw his return to Iowa, which was a return to more familiar circumstances and community. Mary Swander, who was a student of Justice's in the early and middle 1970s, recalls a performance of his poem "Incident in a Rose Garden" for the Writers' Workshop poets. According to her recollection, the players wore wooden masks for the performance, which featured Justice as the Master, Marvin Bell as the Gardener, and Mark Strand as Death. During this period Justice was also playing an ongoing game of chess with Paul Bender. On occasion he would duck into Bender's office, where they would play for twenty minutes or so at a stretch.

Justice continued his experiments with new ways of composing poems. In considering these experiments, it is helpful to bear in mind Wallace Stevens's adage "All poetry is experimental poetry" (1957, 161), which challenges one of the more or less settled orthodoxies of twentieth-century (and now twenty-first-century) American poetry: that there exists a great divide between traditionalists and the avant-garde. Such a divide, or the perception of one, has existed for a long time. One need only think of Ben Jonson's reported statement concerning John Donne's meters, or what Jonson perceived to be the lack thereof: that Donne, "for not keeping of accents, deserved hanging" (5). With his ear classically trained and exquisitely tuned, Jonson could not quite hear what Donne was actually doing. A more recent manifestation of this divide is articulated in Donald M. Allen's preface to his influential anthology *The New American Poetry* (1960), in which he asserts that the poets he includes, who share the common characteristic of a "total rejection of all those qualities typical of academic verse," are "our avant-garde" (xi; see also Perkins 351–53, and Beach 189).

As Stevens's adage attests, however, the opposition between the traditional and the experimental will not hold. Even so stalwart a traditionalist as Yvor Winters emphasized that "experimental poetry may be traditional in many aspects" (84). Such an assertion would no doubt have made sense to T. S. Eliot, who in "Tradition and the Individual Talent" discussed how the new work of art must simultaneously fit into and challenge its tradition. As Eliot put it, "To conform merely would be for the new work not really to conform at all; it would not be new, and would therefore not be a work of art" (1960, 5). The true work of art challenges the very tradition of which it is a part. The tradition stays alive by being thus challenged.

But unfortunately this notion of a great divide between aesthetic allegiances has persisted. As Justice put it in his 1996 interview with Dana Gioia, "internecine struggles" of the poetry world "waste good energy." He pointed out that these struggles had "been going on since I started writing poetry—the poetry wars. I regret the poetry wars" (CS 200). In these wars the Iowa Writers' Workshop was taken as representative of the academic side of the struggle as opposed to such outsider, avant-garde groups as the Beats and the New York School (see Lehman 333–39). Justice represents very well a case of the "academic" poet—one who uses such traditions as rhyme, recognizable meters, and a coherent and relatively unified voice—who is at the same time experimental in his struggle always to make something new. In discussing the "formal experiment" of Justice's poetry, Mark Jarman comments (2002) that "it should come as no surprise that Donald Justice is one of our most experimental poets, and his testing and proving of formal devices have varied widely over the years."

Justice's own comments often defy simple categorization. In an early interview, for example, he described how he once offered a copy of Allen Ginsberg's *Howl* to his student who could write the best sonnet. He explained
that "by rubbing up together," the influences of *Howl* and the sonnet form
"might produce something a little more interesting than either of the two
extremes" (PS 6). His interest in poetry in excess of the familiar categories
shows also in his introduction to *The Collected Poems of Weldon Kees*: "Kees
is original in one of the few ways that matter: he speaks to us in a voice or,
rather, in a particular tone of voice which we have never heard before" (ix).
While Justice recognizes the importance of traditional means and influences
in Kees, he also looks to what is new. The commitment to experiment—with
form, tone, style—shows too in his commentaries about his own work. In
a 1975 interview, he said that he has "wanted, as many poets must have, to
try all kinds of things in writing" and not to be "satisfied with, say, finding a
formula for writing a poem and then doing it a second time, except perhaps
in a short series of related poems, with the end already in sight" (PS 30).
And again: "Certainly you don't want to keep doing the same things over and
over, things you have already done" (ibid., 8).

One of the ways that he kept from repeating himself was by his use of
chance operations to write some of the poems that would appear in *Departures*. Opening his poems to the workings of chance was another way of
depersonalizing the work, of allowing the words on the page to become more
conspicuously things to be manipulated, combined, and recombined. Although with Justice's finely tuned ear, many of these poems seldom stray far
from iambic meter—and many individual lines scan as perfect iambics—these
poems are fairly characterized as free verse. With the lines' variable numbers
of feet and syllables, the frequent shifts away from traditional meter, and the
general abandonment of rhyme, these poems experiment with possibilities
outside the traditional received forms. Again, although there is no necessary
connection between form and subject matter, experimentation can allow a
poet to move into a new "form" in the expansive sense that Justice defines
it in his discussion of "benign obscurity" (1998a, 80–91), whether he is discussing the deployment of various verbal effects that refer "loosely back to
some general mood-center" or the intimation of a narrative using a "high
degree of indirection" (ibid., 85, 89). The notion of "form" that constitutes
"benign obscurity" is the achievement of a "measure of obscurity without the
integrity of the poem being seriously compromised" (ibid., 91). The larger
sense of "form" that many of Justice's poems in *Departures* achieve is a deep-

ly detached and depersonalized tone within circumstantial presentations of a world. As these two tendencies—the presentation of a personal world and the detached tone—develop together, they create a tonal effect of depersonalized intimacy.

One poem that achieves this effect is "Sonatina in Yellow" (CP 166–67), which is concerned largely with the relationship between personal memory and the distancing function of artistic discipline, here represented by the art of photography. While the pages of the photograph album orient the poem to the speaker's past, the poem's opening lines—"The pages of the album, / As they are turned, turn yellow"—create a sense of distance from the past not only by referring to the photograph album, a repository of images, but also by invoking the cinematic effect of a fluttering of pages, conventionally associated with an accelerated passing of time. This focus on the material of memory holds what is remembered at some distance. But the moment of remembering is already over by the time the poem begins. While the photograph album is much associated with a movement into the past, the yellowing of the pages as they turn indicates a forward movement in time. Were the pages taking us backward in time, then they would be losing rather than taking on the yellowing of age. At the opening of the poem, the speaker greets the reader as the former is returning from his journey into the past. There is no question of taking the reader along on this journey, for he can report on his sojourn in personal memory only after the fact. The shadowy realm of the past exists in the traces of memory, and the speaker-poet provides the reader with traces of these traces, for even deeply personal memory remains fragmentary.

The version of a memory that the poem provides is only one among many that the poet could formulate, for a given memory may always be uttered in alternate terms with different implications. Any version conceals as much as it reveals as it also withholds as much as it discloses. Justice's withholding is itself central to his art. In considering the nostalgic emotions in Justice's poetry, William Logan emphasizes that "one of the merits of Justice's poetry lies, not in its absence of emotion, but in its withholding of confidence from emotion" (CS 92). This withholding shows in the speaker's self-command in the opening strophe:

> . . . a word,
> Once spoken, obsolete,
> No longer what was meant. Say it.
> The meanings come, or come back later,
> Unobtrusive, taking their places.

The speaker gives primary confidence not to the emotion, but rather to the act of speaking, as the command "Say it" emphasizes. The material of the language will call forth what remains to emerge. Such meanings as are relevant will arise unobtrusively, in their own time, carrying both speaker and reader to the meanings now grown obsolete. The poet's primary responsibility is the saying, the language, the material of his art. The emergent aesthetic is one of confidence in this material, the language, and the direction it moves when attended to, for the meanings will emerge if one remains disciplined with regard to the act of utterance.

The command "Say it" functions in parallel to the further commands to remember and to forget: "Think of the past. Think of forgetting the past." These two hortatory statements point out the focus of the poem, not so much the remembered event as the dynamics of recollection and forgetting, such dynamics as enable memory to function. With too little recollection, there is no past to narrate; with too much, there is no narrative since the sheer accretion of detail will overwhelm the narrative framework. To function at all adequately, memory requires some framework (for example, growth of the artist, loss of a state of innocence) within which the selected details cohere and make sense.

Within the framework of literary tradition, the work of the poet requires strategic acts of memory and forgetting. To write, one must know—meaning in some sense or other to remember—other poetry. But to work as an artist also means that one cannot simply repeat what is remembered; rather, one must create something new, as Eliot wrote the poet must do. The creative act requires some swerving away from—a kind of strategic forgetting of—the accumulations of tradition (see Bloom 1973, 12–21; 2003, 95–98, 199). Further, the working artist must also find ways of negotiating between personal memory and the depersonalized, because collective, memory of tradition. Justice's melding of these modes of memory—the personal and the collective, the historical, biographical, and literary—results in the at once depersonalized and highly evocative language of "Sonatina in Yellow." The poem's structure and stately language mediate the work of remembering and forgetting, thus wresting the event away from the simpler workings of nostalgia.

As the poem's memory work proceeds, the recalled event is implicated in the mode of reflective rather than restorative nostalgia (see Boym 41–49). The recollection continues to be intertwined with the self-conscious work of memory and forgetting, as the voice of the father

rises
In the familiar pattern of reproof
For some childish error, a nap disturbed,
Or vase, broken or overturned;
Rises and subsides. And you do listen.
Listen and forget. Practice forgetting.

This last line creates a productive ambiguity. On the one hand, it can be read as indicating the action of the "you" (a childhood version of the speaker) addressed in the previous line, so that the two fragments of this final line (of the poem's second strophe) connect with the previous independent clause to produce the sentence "And you do listen, listen and forget, practice forgetting." On the other hand, this line can also be read as consisting of further commands, with the "you" implied, to listen and to forget, to practice forgetting. As both meanings play through the line, what begins as conscious self-discipline—with the speaker addressing himself, or that part of himself most in need of this formation, as "you"—becomes second nature. In the midst of its self-adjuration, the poem emphasizes the training and practice necessary for even the simplest process of remembering well, a process that casts what is remembered in a comprehensible narrative pattern that avoids the degradation of sentimentality. Such a discipline of memory demands the kind of detachment that Justice signals in the description of remembering and forgetting as an "exercise requiring further practice; / A difficult exercise, played through by someone else." Not only is this discipline of remembering and forgetting an art requiring such practice as one might devote to learning a musical instrument, it also requires such distancing from one's intimate feel of selfhood as to seem an exercise "played through by someone else." What is to become second nature begins with self-alienation and only then passes into the habitual texture of one's awareness.

As mentioned above, this poem functions in part as a process of the remembering and the forgetting of literary tradition. In its rhythmically complex and somewhat discursive meditations on time and history, one may hear remote echoes of the Eliot of *Four Quartets*. Having taken up this meditative mode, the speaker reports on his version of the traditional night journey, a visit to the land of the dead. This journey, hinted at by the texture of the poem's details, begins when the voice of the father rises "from the next room still / With all the remote but true affection of the dead." The speaker then enters, in this journey of memory, the land of the dead proper:

> Remember
> The dead air of summer. Remember
> The trees drawn up to their full height like fathers,
> The underworld of shade you entered at their feet.

The details of this passage form an associative complex in which the trees become fathers casting a shade that is the underworld the speaker enters to encounter the memory of his own father. The commands that follow lead the speaker into the underworld realm of the specific memory he has been pursuing:

> Enter the next room. Enter it quietly now,
> Not to disturb your father sleeping there. *He stirs.*

The combination of personal memory with the night journey motif creates the terms of the poem's depersonalized exploration. Like Aeneis in Book Six of the *Aeneid*, the speaker of "Sonatina in Yellow" encounters the shade of his father. But unlike Anchises, who explains to his son the doctrine of metempsychosis, as well as the glories and sorrows to come, the father in Justice's poem does not speak. Or rather, he "*rises*" and "*speaks*," but not for us, the poem's readers. Having split himself into two personae—the one making the night journey and the one leading, the latter of whom addresses the former as "you"—the poem's speaker proceeds on the journey for a purely personal disclosure; what is given to the reader is a delineation of the formal artistic discipline by which such disclosure occurs.

The poem's moment of withholding the father's utterance is characteristic of Justice's restraint. The emphasis here is on the way art creates a framework for memory, as well as the ways that memory issues in further artistic work. At the moment of the father's speaking, the poem immediately returns to the movement of hands over piano keys, an image of technical discipline:

> *He rises, speaks . . .*
>
> Repeat it now, no one was listening.
> So your hand moves, moving across the keys,
> And slowly the keys grow darker to the touch.

What began as a focus on language—the "Say it" of the poem's fourth line—and the unobtrusive meanings "taking their places," ends with reference to pure sound, the music of repeated practice. This image of the isolated, even objectified hands moving across the piano keys emphasizes the kind of technical accomplishment that makes art a fit vehicle for the discipline of memory.

Given the progression of this poem from memory of the father to the pursuit of art, one might also read the final lines' playing as compensation for the loss of the father—a familiar Freudian style of understanding the motive for art (Freud 25–34; see also Sacks 1–18). In playing out his work of counterbalancing the losses of the past, the poet also presents a dialogue between past and present that demonstrates the "struggle of the mind and heart with the welter and fixations of nostalgia" (Bate 131). A poem that plays out this struggle with nostalgia specifically in terms of what Walter J. Bate calls literary history's "accumulating anxiety and the question it so directly presents to the poet or artist: *What is there left to do?*" (3), is Justice's "Sonatina in Green" (CP 164—65). Another of the poems that came out of his experiments with chance methods, this one takes up the question of what it means to be a latecomer in a tradition already characterized by an embarrassment of riches (see Bloom 1973, 12–21). The sense of belatedness that emerges is one that the speaker articulates in terms of a world where the gods and heroes have fallen away. There is no question here of existing in a gold, silver, or bronze age, but rather in something more like the fourth, or iron, age of Ovid's *Metamorphoses*, that is in "no part good and tractable as former ages past" (131). The sonatina's repeated statement—"There has been traffic enough / In the boudoir of the muse"—affirms that the time of intimacy with the divine inspirations of poetry is over. The closing three lines most clearly set out the poem's situation with regard to literary tradition:

Closed are the grand boulevards,
And closed those mouths that made the lesser songs,
And the curtains drawn in the boudoir.

Uncompromising in its view of the present as a falling away from the past, the poem draws the curtains on the scene of intimate traffic with the deities of the sublime. Even the major achievement of minor poetry in the old style—that of "those mouths that made the lesser songs"—lies out of reach. We find ourselves in a decadent age, with the "garland / Crushed at the threshold" and "Smells of decaying greenery, faint bouquets."

Even though the poem alludes to the ancient world of myth, we are a long way from the moment of sublime vision and loss in "The Wall." The poem's opening line epitomizes the younger generation's attitude toward the older mode: "One spits on the sublime." Nor does the poet-speaker hold out hope for the ancient mode, even if something like it were still possible:

> Or say
> That one composed, in the end,
> Another beginning, in spite of all this,
> Sublime. Enough!

A cursory reading might lead one to conclude that the poem has succumbed to an uncomplicated nostalgia for the grandeurs of an inaccessible literary past. Given the poem's dedication, "for my students," it would even seem to teach that because there is already sublime verse enough in the world, those "demanding entrance, / Noisy, and with ecstatic cries" would do well to spend their energies otherwise than on writing poems. However, the poem—in part by its very status as verse—swerves away from such thoroughgoing discouragement even as it puts on display the difficulty of writing in the present, given the great tradition that any artist must negotiate. The poetry goes on, and this sonatina exemplifies a mode of writing responsive to tradition, thus refusing the dodge of idealizing a past that one is condemned either to repeat or to stand before in motionless and mute awe. To remain motionless is to forego any act of creation, and simply to repeat the past is to forego the burdens of creation. The poem holds out for acknowledgment of past greatness, as well as taking on the challenge of entering a living tradition in new terms, forms, and tones of voice. While this sonatina professes that there has been poetry enough in the old mode of the sublime, with its paraphernalia of gods and heroes, it also implies that what one should do in an age of belatedness is write in full acknowledgment of one's belated position and what it means to be a latecomer. The poem embraces its anxiety of influence.

The poem even takes this anxiety as one of its enabling conditions. It is an anxiety that compels creation rather than repetition. By implication, the speaker-poet also adjures his students fully to face the anxieties attendant upon struggling to enter a tradition that does not need them. The question that he asks concerning these noisy and ecstatic young writers is crucial:

> For them, what music? Only,
> Distantly, through some door ajar,
> Echoes, broken strains; and the garland
> Crushed at the threshold.

These distant strains of music constitute what remains in the present of the old mode of muse-inspired poetry. However compelling these distant strains may be, the contemporary poet must find his or her inspiration elsewhere; recall that another poem in *Departures* is "The Telephone Number of the

Muse," in which the speaker recounts his diminishing relationship with the goddess.

The speaker-poet of "Sonatina in Green" teaches primarily by example. He and his contemporaries are now, as the elders of poetry, the caretakers and players of the "old instruments"; and even these elders must face the same question earlier put to the students:

> And we,
> We few with the old instruments,
> Obstinate, sounding the one string—
> For us, what music? Only, at times,
> The sunlight of late afternoon
> That plays in the corner of a room,
> Playing upon worn keys. At times,
> Smells of decaying greenery, faint bouquets—
> More than enough.

Even those in possession of the ancient instruments do not *seem* to play with full virtuosity, but only obstinately sound "the one string." In *The Dismemberment of Orpheus* (1971), Ihab Hassan characterizes the situation of this belated moment as one in which writers must play a lyre without strings. Justice leaves a single string on the ancient Orphic instrument, so that the poet might pluck out a tune somewhat, if only remotely, reminiscent of past modes. The speaker of "Sonatina in Green" feels his contemporary moment as both diminished in its possibilities and awash in the riches of a grand tradition. The question "What is there left to do?" weighs as heavily on him as on his students.

The elders would seem to lack virtuosity only if one expected from them the same kind of music played on the same instruments as the music from the past. Perhaps even in spite of himself, this rather gloomy speaker is playing a new kind of music. As is often the case, the new music—because it differs markedly from the old—may not at first be recognizable as legitimate. So this poet's new song, one that thematizes his latecomer status, is one that even he himself denigrates. The poem exemplifies a kind of paradoxical, even postmodern, sublime, one that depends on the poem's rich refusals—not that the poem is itself sublime (a mode that is no longer available), but rather that it calls up the sublime by denying it. There is after all something marvelous in the muted tones of "sunlight of late afternoon / That plays in the corner of a room, / Playing upon worn keys." In its rich disciplines, its rigorous refusals, the poem demonstrates that in an age of belatedness, the sublime available is that which we have foregone. Like Adam and Eve as they leave the Garden, we may catch a glimpse of the grand image only at the moment of experiencing its loss. "Sonatina in Green" brings us to this moment of loss with great awareness.

Another poem from *Departures* that meditates on the literary situation (though not one that emerged from Justice's experiments with chance methods) is "Homage to the Memory of Wallace Stevens" (CP 162–63). Although the poem pays tribute to one of Justice's great influences, it begins by distancing itself from Stevens by minimizing his importance: "Hartford is cold today but no colder for your absence." The line might be read as a symptom of the anxiety of influence, which seeks to mute the significance of one's strongest precursors. At the same time, the line honors Stevens's poetry by taking seriously his emphasis on the brute facticity of the world, made over by human imagination (see Bloom 1976, 27–35). The world is what is encountered in the daily round of experience; the disappearance of even the most significant of people cannot alter the weather. At the same time, Stevens continues to be associated with artistic practice:

> Nevertheless,
>
> The poet practicing his scales
> Thinks of you as his thumbs slip clumsily under and under,
> Avoiding the darker notes.

Even practicing the scales holds out promise of making the world over into something of great constancy.

The poem's second section carries through with Stevens's implied critique, at the end of "The Man on the Dump," of treating truth as singular. As Justice puts it, "The *the* has become an *a*." The singularity of "the the" has given way to a pluralist vision of "a"—an article signaling one among many possibilities and approaches. In the final line of this brief section, he also signals the passing of Stevens's poetic mode, influenced by French symbolism: "Who borrows your French words and postures now?" This line is the poem's great tour de force, for it echoes syllable by syllable the closing line of Milton's "Lycidas": "Tomorrow to fresh woods and pastures new." "Tomorrow" becomes "Who borrows," as "to fresh woods" becomes "your French words," and "and pastures new" becomes "and postures now." In "Lycidas" Milton is paying tribute to fellow poet Edward King (a classmate of Milton's at Cambridge) who has died, while at the same time furthering his own poetic vocation. Arguably, part of what constitutes the tribute is the continuation of the literary work from which King has been cut off. Justice is doing much the same with his tribute to Stevens, though the echo of Milton places him in the company of that elder poet as well. The echo of the Milton line also signals Justice's commitment to further literary endeavors. The closing line of "Lycidas" is commonly taken to imply Milton's looking ahead to new modes of poetry; having written his pastoral elegy, he was to set out in pursuit of new and more ambitious work, culminating in his great epic. While Justice's line pays tribute to Stevens's "French words and postures" (his literary manners adapted from the French symbolists), the echo of the Milton line also assures that the latter-day poet is looking ahead to "fresh woods and pastures new"—that is, to new ways of writing.

The opening line of section three, "The opera of the gods is finished," signals that the grand, operatic gestures and language, exemplified by such figures as Milton and Stevens (both of them more than credible members of the cast), are of the past. In fact, the "chorus will soon be coming down from the clouds," for now they must inhabit the earth. The very language of the old opera is no longer available, for the only summing up available is the chorus's silence—and even this silence is a "final platitude of sorts." When an older mode is employed past the moment of its liveliness, it becomes the stuff of banality. Even the gesture of silence, in the context of such backward leaning, takes on an air of something stale. It is not that Milton and Stevens are even close to banal, but that trying to imitate their modes of language in the present can only result in literary disaster.

So the old mythic world of the literary gods takes up residence in the more everyday surroundings of a "treeless street." Nevertheless, something remains of the old stories, something of the "pas de deux of Eden," even if the dance is now that of "cotsprings creaking like the sun and moon." The sexual acts that make these springs creak retain after all some cosmic significance. Even if these cotsprings creak like the machinery of a universe whose "operation" is "temporarily suspended," they still retain something of universal meaning, even if this universe is running down.

The poem defers the moment of literary fulfillment, as this moment must be deferred; the life of literature goes on because it remains partial, unfulfilled, in need of further supplement. By asking whether the good and beautiful are embodied in the tuning of the instruments or the putting them away, the poem elides the moment of performance. As is fitting to the sense of the contemporary moment that the poem implies, we are left with the paraphernalia of the old performance but not the performance in the present tense. What remains are the instruments, and what remains to do in the present is to describe this world of belatedness, one in which the instruments "sleep on plush and velvet till / Our breath revives them to new flutterings, new adieux." The promise of new songs to be played on these instruments is crucial, for were they to remain merely on display, they and the history that they represent would become mere curios rather than parts of a living tradition. There must be a promise of new singing, even if the singing is deferred. For the moment the description of the belated moment is the song that will suffice. But even this description already breaks into song—with its iambic lines of variable length and abundance of anapestic substitutions (resembling the meter that Justice associates with Stevens's later style; see "The Free-Verse Line in Stevens," 1998a, 28–37); it signals that more singing is to come. In the announcement of the "new adieux" to the old songs, the new songs have already begun.

Meanwhile, the singers from the opera gather at the picnic. Something like the old gods are still present, it's just that they no longer wear the "golden costumes" of gods. Does the statement that they are "no less gods for that" (for not wearing their costumes) imply that they never were gods to begin with, or that they are gods who simply have given up their status as gods? The former option (which holds that if they never had the status of gods, then they are not giving up any status based in reality) discloses that there never were gods at all, the latter that the existence of the gods is quite complex in the modern world. I suspect that the best reading of the poem resists the either/or proposition. On the one hand, the stage setting of the opera implies that to be a god in this world means to play a role, complete with the proper costuming and choreography. On the other hand, to play such a role well means to be sufficiently godlike to call forth awe. To be a god means to be able to play the role successfully, and of highest importance in the literary world is the ability to write like a god. What is crucial in literature is the text, and in the poem's closing lines we learn that "all quotations from the text apply." These are quotations of "laughter," "offstage thunder," and "this almost human cry." In other words, even if the opera is closed down, one can still encounter its utterances and effects in the text, which still has its own life in the contemporary world. Further, one also encounters this new text that is the "Homage to the Memory of Wallace Stevens," a text whose cry is *almost* human because the voice is depersonalized. But it is in such depersonalized art that one can most powerfully encounter the *techne*, the art, the artifice that discloses to us and challenges who we are as human beings (see Ong 1982, 82–83).

The loss registered in Justice's poems is not limited to the literary situation, but includes the social and political worlds as well, as exemplified in another of his chance-methods poems, "The Assassination" (CP 143). Dated "June 5, 1968," the poem situates itself on the day that Robert Kennedy was shot, which was the day before he died. Describing the genesis of this poem in an interview Justice said: "for the first time I had a television set, so I could see the events in an immediate and scary way. So I thought—I feel something about this; I have something to say about it; maybe this is one of those public events one can write about" (PS 26). The technology of television also had a more direct influence on the poem in that he used words he heard on the televised news reports about the shooting; he wrote them on the cards that he shuffled to generate lines for the poem in his experiments with chance.

There is also in the poem's feel for the Kennedy assassination, mediated by television, an example of what Marshall McLuhan famously referred to as the "new electronic interdependence" that "recreates the world in the image of a global village" (31). Such technology of communication as television can alter one's feeling for events in part by bringing what happens in remote spaces into greater proximity than would otherwise be possible. As Walter Ong, taking up McLuhan's insight, puts it, "Before television no human psyche had experienced visually and aurally events actually going on in the real present but in an extraneous locale" (1977, 316). "The Assassination," by articulating a vision of the Kennedy assassination, registers not only the loss of great promise, but also a sense of the world changing in less obvious though no less real ways. The world becoming a global village alters how one relates to the local village. As television allows one to relate in more circumstantial terms to the former, it also tends to fragment the latter in new ways, creating such anxieties as evidenced by polemics concerning the effects of television (see Postman 83–154). But this estrangement from the familiar works well in relation to Justice's mode of depersonalization. To gain perspective on what is proximate, one needs some distance from it. With its effects of bringing remote events nearer and fragmenting the local, television reconfigures the terms of experiencing the world.

A feeling for the world grown unfamiliar is signaled by the poem's repeated use of *it*, which occurs twelve times in the course of the poem's fifteen lines. As the meaning of this most objective and objectifying of pronouns shifts through the poem, it calls attention to the feeling of alienation from a world perceived as personally threatening:

It begins again, the nocturnal pulse.
It courses through the cables laid for it.

It mounts to the chandeliers and beats there, hotly.
We are too close. Too late, we would move back.
We are involved with the surge.

Whatever "it" is, this unnamed thing has drawn us into its surging force.
The opening line suggests that "it" is a pulse, and since this "nocturnal
pulse" courses through the "cables laid for it," it makes sense to read "it" as
news of the shooting, which has been turned into electrical signals coursing
through the cables bringing news to television sets around the world. Justice
himself identified the central image as blood, which *runs* all through the
poem" (PS 26). The intentional fallacy notwithstanding (see Wimsatt 3–18),
it seems reasonable to take Justice's suggestion, because this news is bloody
indeed, as reinforced by the word, *pulse*, that ends the first line.

The bloody news courses through all the locales of the world touched
by the televised reports. The experience of the events in Los Angeles is
brought into proximity, and it is too late to "move back" either in the sense
of disengaging from the urgency and immediacy of the news, or in the sense
of moving back to a time before the new technologies (radio, television)
remade the world into fragmented spaces drawn together in a complex and
depersonalized global village. Once a culture becomes powerfully altered
by new communications technologies, it becomes impossible to return to a
state of seeming innocence before the cultural shifts took place. The shifts
in meaning of the pronoun *it* register the complexity of this world, as "it"
can variously refer to electricity, the tragic news that television delivers, the
blood of the bloody news, the altered sense of the world brought on by this
news (one among several prominent deaths of the 1960s that contributed to
a feeling of innocence lost), and the altered sense of the world brought on by
the new technology. These multiple meanings circulate through the poem as
the pronoun recurs.

In the poem's third strophe, the speaker finds himself in the presence of
this ambiguous "it." Fittingly for this poem of encountering the impersonal
in personal terms, the most circumstantial and intimate moment—the one
in which the speaker opens his arms to "it"—is the one in which he is drawn
into the remote locale of the events taking place in Los Angeles:

Here is the red marquee it sheltered under,
Here is the ballroom, here
The sadly various orchestra led
By a single gesture. My arms open.
It enters. Look, we are dancing.

The speaker enters the ballroom where Kennedy delivered his speech before he was shot while taking a shortcut through the hotel kitchen. The death of this young and promising leader puts in the air a sense of death that connects with and complicates the feeling of the death of an older, more unified feeling of the world. But this unified world sense can be experienced only in retrospect, for it is a cultural nostalgia that this speaker resists. By the end of the poem, the third-person pronoun also comes to refer to death itself; thus, the final line creates a modernized version of the Danse Macabre, or Dance of Death, that signals here the speaker coming to his own terms with the larger tragedy taking place.

The tradition of the Danse Macabre probably goes back to medieval sermons on death. The pictorial representations of the dance were initially images of a decomposing corpse, representing the dead man (the figure was usually male) himself. Later, the dancer became the figurative representation of Death as a skeleton, who was followed by a grave procession of Death's captives (White IX–IV). The life (as it were) of the Danse Macabre continued in response to events of the twentieth century, such as in the drawings of Frans Masereel's *Danse Macabre* (1942). Of particular relevance to "The Assassination" is Fritz Eichenberg's *Dance of Death: A Graphic Commentary on the Danse Macabre through the Centuries* (1983), which has a photograph of a 1970 photo-silkscreen by Robert Rauschenberg titled "Signs" (97) that includes images of John F. Kennedy, Martin Luther King, Jr., and Robert Kennedy.

In Justice's version of the Dance of Death, in which the speaker of "The Assassination" dances with Death in the ballroom, the dance involves moving with the various senses of death that I have pointed out in relation to the poem, from the death that comes as a result of the shooting to the death of an older, more familiar sense of the world. This dance affirms the importance of art—for example, the arts of both dance and poetry—in response to tragedy and confusion. The speaker's dance has him engaging with rather than evading the recent events. He encounters the remote events in the intimate, tactile, proprioceptive terms of dancing. Throughout the poem he has articulated his uneasiness with the "it" that eventually becomes his dancing partner. His final exclamation—"Look, we are dancing"—calls attention to his nervousness and even surprise at himself thus engaging with the recent events and what they mean.

Justice's chance methods constitute only one example of how he experimented with depersonalization. Perhaps his most ironically and dramatically depersonalized poem—though one that did not arise from chance methods—is "Poem" (CP 160–61). The irony arises from the way the poem directly addresses the reader while it also refuses the reader's relevance to the poem, as well as the poem's relevance to the reader. But the more the poem pushes against the reader, the more compelling it becomes. In keeping with Justice's depersonalized and objective stance, "Poem" functions as an example of what J. Hillis Miller calls the "linguistic moment," which occurs "when language itself is foregrounded and becomes problematic" (1985, 41). This foregrounding of language calls attention to the poem's "textual condition," which means that as a material text, it calls into play ambiguous roles of writer and reader, both of whom enter into complex relations with the physical text, and whose interactions create the text's meaning (see McGann 88–98).

Justice's linguistic moment begins,

> This poem is not addressed to you.
> You may come into it briefly,
> But no one will find you here, no one.
> You will have changed before the poem will.

In addressing the absent reader concerning the very poem under way, the speaker displaces both reader and poem, calling attention to the constant displacements that constitute acts of reading and writing (see Derrida 68). The material text—the words and sentences and lines on the page—is never quite the text as fantasized, idealized, or conceived. Recall again Justice's conception of the "Platonic script" functioning as a heuristic device for his writing. The notion of the Platonic text that exists before the act of writing enables the poet to gather language to form a seeming whole that turns out to be fragmentary, a falling away from the fantasized Platonic ideal. In recognition of its condition as a swerve away from its impossible ideal form, "Poem" articulates its own absence as much as it announces its presence: "It has been most beautiful in its erasures." This is not exactly Derridean erasure—the use of a necessary term with a recognition of the term's inaccuracy or errancy (see Spivak's preface in Derrida xiii–xviii)—though there is considerable overlap in that both Derridean erasure and Justice's line refer to the partiality and inadequacy of the available terms. Similarly, Justice's Platonic ideal remains an enabling though self-admittedly errant point of reference. It is Platonism under erasure. "Poem" partakes of Justice's mode of writing in compensation for what is lost, or for what never was. His Platonism under erasure admits itself as unreal even as it functions as an impossible ideal that allows the imperfect and compelling poem to come to be. As a text shimmering with the ideal text that it refers to and defers, "Poem" becomes a kind of forlorn literary suburb with a golden name.

The poem also calls attention to the shifting, ambiguous, and fictive role that the reader must play. For example, the opening line, in provoking the reader's entry into the text by an outright denial, casts the reader in a role of detached and spurned observer who is nevertheless goaded into reading on. As Walter Ong points out in "The Writer's Audience Is Always a Fiction," the reader of a given text "has to play the role in which the author has cast" him or her. Ong continues: "a history of the way audiences have been called on to fictionalize themselves would be a correlative of the history of literary genres and literary works, and indeed of culture itself" (1977, 60–61; see also Stewart 3–28). The complex role that the reader of Justice's "Poem" is called on to play is one cognizant of the textual condition of intersecting mediations and how the reader's implied roles will shift. This is a reader who "may come into" the poem, however "briefly" but always self-consciously, insofar as reading means entering a text and giving it life, for without the reader a text remains but marks on a page. Whatever effect, as well as affect, the poem has is that which the reader supplies in response to its provocations. For what feeling does the text have without the reader? "Poem" itself supplies the answer: "It is not sad, really, only empty." If the poem is to be sad, it must be so as a result of a reader experiencing sadness in relation to the text.

At the same time, even as the reader supplies such affect, the marks on the page remain unchanged, and thus "no one will find you here, no one." Even if such a reader/writer as Coleridge—whose marginalia have entered literary history and tradition—manages to mark pages in such a way as to catch many readers' attention, these traces are no more the presence of the reader/annotator than "Poem" is the presence of the poet. Whatever annotations a reader might inscribe enter circuits of realization and become as subject to the playing of fictive roles as does "Poem." As much reader-response criticism has pointed out with great nuance, the meaning that comes from negotiating a text does not *reside* in the writer, text, or reader, but rather *emerges* from their interaction. Meaning does not reside at all, for meaning is an event (see, for example, Iser).

"Poem" provokes an exquisite awareness of meaning as event. Responses to it have produced a highly self-conscious and at times even agonized mode of commentary, for it disrupts such complacent notions of meaning as are far too easy to sink into. For example, Gerald Bruns responds to "Poem": "Can't you see that it simply wishes to be rid of me, the common and gentle reader, and so it conspires with certain handy devices to disguise my presence? I am the you in the poem who is not addressed, and who is therefore abolished as by creating discourse" (72). Reading "Poem" means playing the role of one who is both addressed and put off, one who is rejected, scorned, irrelevant—at least in the sense that older modes of reading, as in the manner of the "gentle reader" of older-fashioned address, are no longer relevant. Picking up on the sheer strangeness of the text, Jerome McGann writes that "this is the silence of the Sphinx, the analyst's reticence, the priest's reserve" (CS 245). Calling attention to the complex circuits of interaction involved in texts and the generation of their meanings—processes that can be elaborately described but never brought fully into consciousness—strikes into realms of mystery and the sacred. It is commonplace that in societies where literacy is relatively new, and therefore not yet rendered quite familiar, writing is associated with "secret and magic power" (Ong 1982, 93). The complex and often mysterious ways that texts work—even after these ways have been interiorized—may be one reason why among the sacred objects of many traditions, texts play a prominent role, and not only in the religions of the book (Judaism, Christianity, and Islam). One need only read the poems and fictions of Jorge Luis Borges to see how interactions with texts retain a sense of the miraculous if not magical even after literacy has been deeply interiorized. Some residue of the miraculous continues to be associated with text, especially a text so highly self-conscious as "Poem."

By removing language from its immediate discursive context and allowing it to circulate with relative lack of constraint, the printed text bears a pointed relationship to the passing of time, for by removing language from the face-to-face event of the spoken word, the passing of time comes more explicitly into consciousness—the utterance perdures past the situation that generated it. Here is Bruns again: "I was one time the handsome contemporary of this poem, but now you will hardly recognize me. No doubt I am restored now and again to regular sources of dignity, but the poem remains itself, aristocratically reserved" (71). It is in large part this aristocratic reserve that calls forth Bruns's nuanced meditations on the relationships of text and reader to the movements of time. Indeed, "You will have changed before the poem will," and the change is what piques Bruns's attention. As long as there remains a printed page, even though it might tear or turn yellow, "Time's winged chariot" hurries near human consciousness in a way that does not hurry the poem. With regard to the movement of time, Mark Jarman states that "Poem" is an "elegy for [Justice's] reader," though he also remarks that the poem is "a singular recognition of the inevitable effacement of a poet's readers and hence of his work and himself" (1984, 105–6). Here is a further sense in which Justice takes up Eliot's idea that writing a poem is an act of self-effacement.

"Poem" plays off the idea of the text's immortality—see, for example, Shakespeare's "Sonnet 18": "So long as men can breathe or eyes can see, / So long lives this, and this gives life to thee." The former begins by invoking the tradition of textual immortality by implying the poem's stability: "You have begun to vanish. And it does not matter. / The poem will go on without you." But then through the course of the text, it calls subtle attention to its own instability by alluding to its dependence on its readers. As the poem continues to imply, without a reader it remains merely marks on a page. It further registers its instability and ambiguity by referring to itself as the text under discussion while also referring to the text under discussion as something other than what one encounters on the page: "It has been most beautiful in its erasures." It both evokes and withholds: "Listen, it comes without guitar." There is of course no guitar in these printed marks, but the negation of a guitar inevitably carries plenty of guitar associations, as the denial of the guitar includes the word *guitar*.

After six quatrains of evocative withholding, the poem allows two exclamations: "O bleached mirrors! Oceans of the drowned!" Following, as it does, the line about the beauty of erasures, this line delivers images *of* erasure: bleached-out mirrors and lives erased by drowning. And what of these drowned, those who are no longer with us, and the bleached surfaces that once might have reflected their images? The narrative that would tell about them remains suppressed. The only traces of their story are the two exclamations. The suppressed tales are all the more poignant for the poem's restraint. The two brief exclamations are traces of an older mode of writing—something of the High Romantic mode that is a central part of Justice's tradition—functioning under erasure now.

After these exclamations, the poem returns to its intimations of textuality:

Nor is one silence equal to another.
And it does not matter what you think.
This poem is not addressed to you.

As "Poem" demonstrates, the processes of writing and reading involve multiple acts of self-effacement and self-creation. By playing the role that the text calls on me to play—whether as reader or writer—I must give up something of my habitual self. The poem can exist meaningfully only within the space, at once intimate and impersonal, of its fictionalizing webs. As readers and writers, we must enter these webs as well. With his restless creativity, Justice constantly found new ways of weaving texts.

5 ARTISTIC DISCLOSURES

Asked in a 1975 interview what was to come after *Departures*, Justice responded that he was looking ahead to trying something new as well as more traditionally formal (PS 41). This chapter therefore emphasizes his later experiments with meter, as well as how the formal disciplines of art enable an understanding of the world. Meter is only one of the many formal disciplines by which humans have gathered their experiences, perceptions, and insights into organized modes of discourse. As Robert K. Logan points out in *The Extended Mind* (2007), a word is a "strange attractor" for a variety of experiences and "therefore, packs a great deal of experience into a single utterance or sign" (45). Much of Justice's later work discloses how our artistic forms and traditions encode and carry arrays of human experience, which become available to the initiate in the art.

The years following 1975 brought for Justice a variety of experiments with traditional meters, beginning with the newer pieces in the "Uncollected Poems" section of the *Selected Poems* (1979)—which won the Pulitzer Prize—and extending through the "New Poems" section of the *Collected Poems* (2004). In the meantime, other honors came his way; in 1976 he was the Brain-Swiggert Lecturer at Princeton University, as well as a Guggenheim Fellow in poetry.

Justice found out that he was the recipient of the Pulitzer Prize in a rather unusual way. In April 1980 he was in Chicago's O'Hare Airport, where he had run into his friend Kim Merker. They heard two announcements over the public address system: the first informed them that because of the snowstorm in progress, the flight they were scheduled to take to Iowa was canceled; the second said that Donald Justice had a telephone call. He had already, in December of 1979, been informed that *Selected Poems* was under consideration for the Pulitzer; the call to O'Hare confirmed that he had won. Although the night was too inclement for air travel, Justice and Merker were able to get seats on a bus bound for Iowa City. One of them had a deck of playing cards, the other a flask. As it turned out, their bus was equipped with small tables, so they traveled through the snowy night celebrating with drinks and games of cards.[1]

Some of the traditionally formal poems to appear in the "Uncollected Poems" section of the prize-winning book returned to Justice's earlier work. One of these was an alternative version of "Anniversaries," the opening poem of the 1960 book *The Summer Anniversaries*. This "new" version, which now bore the title of the book in which it had earlier appeared, is dated 1955, so it might be an earlier draft that he returned to at the time he was putting *Selected Poems* together. In the version published earlier, the emphasis of the scene is on the young boy's scar "Dividing [him] from life." In the 1979 version, we get a different recollection of being "wheeled in a chair" at ten (presumably after the operation for osteomyelitis)

> Until I thought it absurd
> For anyone to have quarreled
> Ever with such a world—
> O brave new planet!—
> And with such music in it. (Justice 1979, 114)

Here he echoes Miranda's cry of wonder in Shakespeare's *Tempest*—"O brave new world/That has such people in't" (5.1.183–84), which he would later allude to in his essay, "A Miranda's World," about his student days in the Writers' Workshop. The music that the boy finds so wondrous on this "brave new planet" is that which he hears proceeding in the world around him:

> The simple voice of a bird
> Or a housewife from her yard
> Flowering in my ear. (Justice 1979, 114)

Already in his perception, the world blooms into art.

Of the newer poems that appear in the *Selected Poems*, Justice has left a rather elaborate account of one of them: "On Writing 'First Death'" (PS 163–67). He recalled beginning work on this poem—about the death of his paternal grandmother, whose funeral was the first he ever attended—in the summer of 1973. At the time he started the poem, he had been sick for a period of some months and, feeling guilty for not writing, began "typing out tetrameter couplets about nothing in particular" (163). Later, looking over these typescripts and trying to recall the precise genesis of the poem, he conjectured that because he usually did not *type* first drafts, he must have been merely exercising, trying to get started again. By the middle of the first page, an image emerged—"raindrops caught in a spiderweb on a back porch" (163)—that he recognized from his childhood visits to his grandparents' farm. Although this image did not survive in the poem, it was enough to get him started.

The verse line that he used in "First Death" (CP 178–80)—"I saw my grandmother grow weak"—comes from "Milton's great pair of poems" (PS 165), "L'Allegro" and "Il Penseroso." The advantage of this line is its inherent flexibility, for one can regard the line as either iambic or trochaic by dropping or adding an initial syllable: "in other words, the first foot is free" (166). Justice's opening line inaugurates the poem's metrical complexity, for the first two feet are perfectly iambic, but then the latter two substitute a different rhythm, yielding (to my ear) the following scansion: "Ĭ sáw | mў gránd | mŏthĕr grów wéak." While the second syllable of *grandmother* carries a secondary stress, in the context of this line, where the word is followed by two strong monosyllables, the latter equalize the second and third syllables of *grandmother*, yielding the above scansion. Thus, the first two iambic feet are followed by what might conventionally be called a pyrrhic foot (two unaccented syllables) and a spondaic foot (two accented syllables). Because a pyrrhic foot is rather rare in English unless it precedes a spondee, I follow Robert Wallace's practice of identifying this configuration as a double iamb (two unaccented syllables followed by two accented syllables), which counts as two feet (Wallace 26–28). The second line then clips the first syllable, yielding a line that begins and ends with an accent and alternates unaccented syllables within the line: "Whén | shĕ diéd, | Ĭ kíssed | hĕr chéek."

The whole poem then shifts, as do Milton's "L'Allegro" and "Il Penseroso," between these two basic metrical patterns. While some of the shorter lines, especially those beginning with prepositional phrases (for example, "From the woods there came a cry"), could credibly be read as consisting of three feet (an anapest followed by two iambs), they may be read just as credibly as the kind of shortened tetrameter line that I have described. Given their occurrence within a poem that is otherwise iambic tetrameter, reading these variant lines as shortened tetrameter becomes more credible. The poem's ending illustrates the dynamic well, with its three perfect iambic tetrameter lines leading to the closing line of clipped tetrameter:

Thĕre wás | ă búz | zĭng ón | thĕ síll.
Ĭt stópped, | ănd éve | rўthíng | wăs stíll.

Wĕ bówed | oŭr heáds, | wĕ clósed | oŭr éyes
Tó | thĕ mér | cў óf | thĕ flíes.

The final-line variation places a particular emphasis on this closing, with its echo of Dickinson's "I Heard a Fly Buzz" and its disturbing implications concerning the "decay that awaits the body in the grave" (Ferlazzo 50). The implicit recognition of the dead body as carrion is all the more striking in the context of the poem's recounting of details of family devotion—for example, "Down the hallway, on its table, / Lay the family's great Bible." Even with all of the assurances of the hereafter, it is here in the world that the child of the poem must learn to live.

In using this form—rhymed couplets and a flexible iambic tetrameter line—for "First Death," Justice may have unconsciously hit upon a convention that in the twentieth century came to be associated with the elegy. It is the meter that Seamus Heaney used in his elegy for Joseph Brodsky, "Audenesque." As Heaney explained, the meter is one that Auden used in the third section of his elegy for Yeats, "In Memory of W. B. Yeats," and that Yeats used in "Under Ben Bulben," in which he anticipates his own death.[2] Both Heaney's and Auden's examples hew to the seven-syllable line quite strictly. Justice's poem echoes more the shifting line of Yeats, as well as that of Milton.

Also among the new poems in *Selected Poems* was "Childhood," discussed in chapter 1 in relationship to Justice's complex view of the past. This complexity comes to the fore most strikingly in "Thinking about the Past" (CP 188), which begins rather strangely for this poet of reflective nostalgia: "Certain moments will never change nor stop being." At first glance the line seems to be a denial that the past is really past at all, affirming rather that it goes on existing in some eternal and changeless realm. What can it mean that these changeless moments will not stop being? A hint of an answer comes in line five: "All fixed into place now, all rhyming with each other." The past must be made to rhyme, submitted to the rigors of art, to last. These details of the past will perdure, in other words, insofar as they have been transformed into art. The poem here affirms what Justice wrote in his essay on "First Death," that such technical devices as meter and rhyme help to "*fix* the poem, as the right solution fixes the snapshot" (PS 167). He takes up the metaphor again in his essay "Meters and Memory," where he writes that such "artifices are, let us say, the fixatives. Like the chemicals in the darkroom, they are useful in developing the negative" (ibid., 170). Thus, certain moments will not stop being insofar as they have been fixed by some artistic discipline.

But a photograph may fade or be destroyed, and the poem also implies the fragility of what has been "fixed" by art. To begin with, art is only able to fix fragments into place, and it is fragments that the poem delivers: "My mother's face"; Eleanor's "freckled shoulders, hands"; the "breast of Mary Something." It might even be more accurate to call these, rather than "Certain moments," *fragments* of certain moments. But the two lines that most powerfully signal the fragility of what is "fixed" by art are those that recount, one after the other, the tendency for things to lose their structure, to fall into disharmony: "The rock wall building, built, collapsed then, fallen;/Our upright loosening downward slowly out of tune." The instruments of art are themselves as subject to dissolution as the rest of the world. The poem fittingly ends with a run of fragments, the last of which is the "ends of songs . . ." (ellipsis included). As the upright piano cannot but loosen downward, so songs are always ending, as they must, for sound exists only in its evanescence (Ong 1982, 32), as each moment exists only when it is passing away. More than anything else, "Thinking about the Past" recognizes and even celebrates—in its commemorative and fragmentary mode—the passing of time; it fixes this sense of constant passing by using such artistic devices as rhyme, off-rhyme, and meter. Fittingly, the poem ends with an ellipsis, which does not rhyme with anything, implying that there is always more that art cannot fix into place.

Nor did Justice himself stay put. In the early 1980s, he left the University of Iowa. The University of Florida hired him in 1981 on a delayed appointment, so that he could spend a final year teaching at Iowa before taking up new duties in the state of his birth. A note to Paul Engle (March 10, 1982) reveals him finishing up his work at Iowa: "I've passed on the names of Langland and Hecht to Connie, to pass on to Jack, whom I don't see much of these days. Naturally I endorse them, and I hope my endorsement will not have the negative effect it seems to have had on prospects for the job created by my departure. I don't really think it will, but one Never knows." The names that he mentions here are surely those of Joseph Langland, Anthony Hecht, and Connie Brothers, the latter of whom was and as of this writing continues to be the executive assistant of the Writers' Workshop. Niece of the American expatriate poet Robert Lax, Brothers has seen the workshop through some of its most vigorous and productive years.

A note (August 10, 1982) from Justice to Engle and his wife, Hualing, describes the new living situation in Gainesville, Florida: "It actually does resemble the picture on the front hereabouts, though our yard, abutting the university golf course, is greener, even in this very warm summer. We find ourselves looking forward to <u>winter,</u> which is more than most Iowans can say!" The Justices had moved to a neighborhood called Golfview, the setting of Don's poem "Children Walking Home from School through Good Neighborhood." Sometimes golf balls hit the roof and sometimes they wound up in the yard. As William Logan recalled, a "basket of golf balls sat on a table in the entryway, like mints for departing guests" (CS 165). The house was shaped like a boxy U. In one arm of the U was Jean's office, where she wrote fiction; in the other was Donald's office, which also connected to a room that he used as a painting studio.

At the time that Justice arrived at Florida, the only other writer with a national reputation associated with the writing program was Harry Crews. With such satirical novels as *Karate Is a Thing of the Spirit* (1971) and *Car* (1972)—in the latter of which a man agrees to eat a whole car in public, piece by tiny piece, each of which he excretes to be molded into a souvenir for sale—Crews displayed a sensibility that was quite different from that of Justice. They were soon joined, however, by Justice's former students, the poets William Logan and Debora Greger, along with the fiction writer Padgett Powell.

After the publication of his fourth full-length collection, *The Sunset Maker* (1987)—which includes two stories, a memoir, and twenty-five new poems (several of which are composed of sections each of which could stand on its own)—more recognition came his way. He was elected as a fellow of the Academy of American Poets in 1988; in 1991 he was cowinner, with Laura Riding, of the Bollingen Prize; in 1992 he was elected to the American Academy of Arts and Letters, as well as to the position of chancellor of the Academy of American Poets. Further selections of his work appeared: *A Donald Justice Reader* (1991), *New and Selected Poems* (1995), and a British selected poems, *Orpheus Hesitated beside the Black River* (1998).

But there were difficulties also. In the winter of 1990, he suffered a mild heart attack and underwent bypass surgery. Having already been considering retirement, he was able, given a sabbatical, to teach only two semesters during his final three years of employment (CS 167). In late August 1991, he reported that he had "more energy" but then went on: "And that's good, since I met my first class last night. They seemed like a very agreeable lot. Even so, I can't help looking forward to the time when I will be able to stop."[3]

The longing to preserve something of the past, along with a recognition of the near impossibility of doing so, recurs strongly in Justice's writing around this time. A telling example is the following fragment "from the draft of a story" that he used as the epigraph to *A Donald Justice Reader* (1991): "Yet I do not doubt the existence somewhere—in the atmosphere, let us say—of a sort of eternity of sounds. I am told there are scientific grounds to believe this. And in this eternity of sounds Eugene's rich, exact notes persevere. They continue, they repeat themselves, they endure—a form of energy, pure energy of the pure spirit." The complication in this fantasy of an "eternity of sounds" is that even if such sounds exist, they can scarcely be perceived; the fragment continues, "I cannot hear them, or many of them, but I believe they are there. . . ." Nor does it disclose which of these sounds the narrator might be able to hear. Even if they still exist, they remain for the most part beyond perception.

The "Eugene" whose "rich, exact notes" this fragment commemorates is surely Eugene Bestor, Justice's fictitious, minor composer who figures in the story "Night, Death, Etc." and the dramatic monologue "The Sunset Maker" (CP 234–35). This poem is a meditation on transience constantly hinting at something more. Further than other of Justice's poems, this one confronts art's inability to make the transient permanent, though it can record its passing—and the literary "fixing" of ephemerality is as close as we are likely to come to any state of permanence. As the poem's first lines describe, the poem's speaker has inherited the remains of his friend's lifelong devotion to art. But even these remains are not likely to stay in his possession:

> The Bestor papers have come down to me.
> I would suppose, though, they are destined for
> The quiet archival twilight of some library.

The phrase "archival twilight" captures especially well the precarious state of preservation. Ideally, the archive should make these papers available; however, if this twilight fades into darkness, then the papers might as well not exist. If they are ignored entirely, they are as good as lost. The whole poem is haunted by phrases suggestive of endings, loss, and grief: "flags of mourning," "ghost-music," "doomed blossoms," "the fates," "one ghostly phrase."

The speaker wonders at the possibility that something of his friend remains in this archive, so he reads the music and hears "the sounds the notes intend":

> (Some duo of the mind produces them,
> Without error, ghost-music materializing;
> Faintly, of course, like whispers overheard.)

Here he gets at a dynamic of art and what it fixes into place, what it memorializes. Truly to exist, the work of art must be encountered by one who understands; such is the "duo of the mind" that produces not only the music the notes intend, but the words of the poem as well. To overhear the whispers of the dead, one must create the words by active reading. The artists of the past depend on the living to continue the work of reading, performing, interpreting their work; without the work of reading in its multiple forms, there is a fundamental sense in which the artworks themselves cease to exist.

Further, the readers of the present create new works by the new combinations and syntheses that they produce. In his essay on "First Death," Justice points out that with a "'creative' critic something might even be added" (PS 167). If his quotation marks around *creative* register some level of suspicion of what the creative critic might add, no such hesitation holds back the speaker of "The Sunset Maker," who has associated a fragment of Bestor's music with Bonnard's *The Terrace*, which hung in the gallery where the music was performed one day:

> One phrase the cello had, one early phrase,
> That does stay with me, mixed a little now
> With Bonnard's colors.

As a reader he performs what Eliot wrote the well-equipped poet does in "amalgamating disparate experience" (247). For our speaker, Bonnard's colors and Bestor's musical phrase are in a process of becoming a single whole—as, by the poem's final lines, the music, the sound of the gulls, sunset, and Bonnard's colors are combining to form one perceptual pattern, a single gestalt. The speaker's acts of interpretation are keeping Bestor's art alive by entwining it with his own perceptions of the world.

Related to the relationship of the "reader" to the work is that of the artist himself (Bestor) to the reader (the poem's speaker). Does something of Bestor survive in the six notes that function as part of the poem? On the one hand, the speaker would seem to refuse the possibility, for "It's sentimental to suppose my friend / Survives in just this fragment." Besides, he has already affirmed, along with Stravinsky, that to be music it must be abstract. Nevertheless, he holds out the possibility, or at least the question,

> But what if a phrase *could* represent a thought—
> Or feeling, should we say?—without existence
> Apart from the score where someone catches it?

Again, the kind of phrase he refers to here is music, which he has already declared to be abstract, that is, nonrepresentational. And while it remains an overstatement of the case to say that Bestor survives in this tone row fragment, the poem affirms that there is nevertheless something to the idea, something that will not cease to haunt the speaker's imagination, as the fragment haunts his memory: "Falling asleep, I hear it. It is just there. / I don't say what it means." He does not specify whether he will not say or cannot say, but leaves us with the merest suggestion that there may be some way that Bestor survives in this musical phrase—his years of study and discipline, the "perfect ear, the technique, the great gift."

True to his vocation, Justice was deeply interested in the subtle effects of language. For example, in "The Prose Sublime," he analyzes what it is about certain passages of relatively plain prose (as distinct from purple prose or writing of a self-consciously experimental kind) that make them successful in producing "pleasure of the very kind to which poetry is normally thought to have first claim" (1998a, 44). In "Of the Music of Poetry," his concern is with the issue of imitative sound effects, the idea that the sounds of poetry alone (apart from the denotations of the words) can suggest, for example, spaciousness, softness, or bewilderment. Justice had little patience for this critical commonplace. In this regard, he sided with John Crowe Ransom and, in fact, with Dr. Johnson (1977, 547–49). His position was not that sound does not matter in poetry, but rather that it matters much more deeply than can be accounted for by the somewhat desperate notion that sound alone can suggest—except in the most obvious instances of onomatopoeia (for example, buzz, hiss)—what, as it happens, a given line means by the denotations of the words. He was fond of quoting, as he does in "Of the Music of Poetry" (1998a, 77), Ransom's critique of a reading of the line from Edna St. Vincent Millay's poem "Portrait," "Comfort, softer than the feathers of its breast." Elizabeth Atkins, the critic whom Ransom is discussing, comments that with the "many *f*'s and *r*'s and *th*'s a fine feeling of fluffiness is given to [the] line by the many unaccented syllables," so that the line "sounds as soft as the bird's downy breast feels" (239). Ransom responds with a turn of wit to make the point that Justice endorses:

> But I will substitute a line which preserves all these factors and departs from the given line mainly by rearrangement:
>   Crúmpets for the fóster-fáthers of the bráts.
> Here I miss the fluffiness and the downiness. (97)

The idea is that the sounds of Millay's line "suggest" fluffiness and downiness only because these qualities are being described. Change the denotation of the line, and the perceived suggestions of the sounds shift with them. Ransom seems to have taken a rhetorical lesson from Johnson, who critiques Pope's idea, in the *Essay on Criticism*, "The *Sound* must seem an *Eccho* to the *Sense*" (Pope, line 365). As Johnson (1977, 548) points out, one of the "most successful attempts" at imitative sound effects is Pope's description, in his translation of the *Odyssey*, of Sisyphus rolling his boulder up the hill in the Underworld:

> With many a weary step, and many a groan,
> Up a high hill he heaves a huge round stone;
> The huge round stone, resulting with a bound,
> Thunders impetuous down, and smokes along the ground.

Johnson asks, "Who does not perceive the stone to move slowly upward, and roll violently back?" But here is the rub: to "set the same numbers [metrical pattern] to another sense":

> While many a merry tale, and many a song,
> Cheered the rough road, we wished the rough road long.
> The rough road then, returning in a round,
> Mocked our impatient steps, for all was fairy ground.

Johnson's witticism serves to undo the spell of the supposed sound effects: "We have now surely lost much of the delay, and much of the rapidity" (1977, 548).

While Justice agrees with the critiques leveled by Ransom and Johnson, he follows up with reflections of characteristic sensitivity to the workings of language, for there may be something more to the issue: "And yet perhaps there is something in all this imagined correspondence of sound and sense, even though for the most part, when examined in bald detail, it is clearly naïve and unrealistic, based on the sort of simple faith poets are not backward in encouraging, that they are wizards of the language, in control of matters more properly ascribed to chance" (1998a, 77).

In this sentence the neat and expected binaries—correspondence/disparity; wizardly control/sheer chance—break open, hinting at how the opposed terms may intersect, or even at how neither term in either opposition quite applies, allowing subtler notions to emerge. The opening "And yet perhaps," with its multiple warnings, puts us on notice that we are entering some difficult terrain, and that we should abandon naïveté as we proceed. Whatever the as-yet-unnamed "something in all this imagined correspondence" might turn out to be, it will not be the "naïve and unrealistic" version. At the same time, if poets are "not backward in encouraging" the notion of verbal wizardry, neither should they be exactly forward in encouraging the idea—otherwise, there would be no need for the litotes just quoted. So what is there in the idea of imitation to affirm?

The naïve and unrealistic version of imitation yields to a subtler kind of congruence, such as one encounters in the essay "Philip Larkin's Poem 'Com-ing'" (Justice 1998a, 111–15). Justice points out that the repetition in lines ten and eleven—"It will be spring soon,/It will be spring soon"—"exerts some odd slight power" (ibid., 113). Although Justice reminds his reader that he is "constitutionally suspicious" of imitative sound effects in poems, he also admits that once he lets his guard down, he sees "what should have been obvious from the start and doubtless has always been so to others. The repeated line is an imitation of the thrush's song, faint perhaps, as all such imitative effects are, but true. Not that it intends, of course, to reproduce the actual sounds of the bird's song, but only to stand in for it in a poem by way of a familiar and unexpressed convention" (ibid., 113–14). It isn't that the convention assimilates the natural world, but rather that it creates its own realm. This realm of artifice then, by its own means, echoes and alludes to the natural world. We get to the moment of congruence by way of artifice and convention.

The poems in *The Sunset Maker* continued Justice's experiments with the possibilities of traditional forms. In much of this work, he was tapping into one of the main sources of poetry's rhetorical strength, the flexible verse line. One of the most powerful ways that this line functions rhetorically is by calling attention to and stressing words, phrases, and lines where metrical substitutions and variations occur. The distinction between the former and the latter is important for the present considerations (see Brooks and Warren 119–31, and Shapiro 61–76). A substitution replaces one kind of metrical foot with another—for example, the replacement of an iamb with a trochee (perhaps the most common substitution in English practice). A variation modulates the rhythm of a given foot without altering the meter. The effect of a variation is created by a number of means, from the relative balancing of the syllables in a foot (so that they are barely distinguishable from each other, though still enough so to allow the recognizable meter to take effect) to the insertion of a breath pause between syllables. Some examples from Justice's earlier practice should prove helpful.

In "The Wall" (CP 13) (see chapter 1) the opening line—"Thĕ wáll | sŭrroúnd | ĭng thém | thĕy név | ĕr sáw"—establishes the iambic pentameter. The second line introduces variations in the second and third feet: "Thĕ án | gĕls, óf | tĕn. Án | gĕls wére | ăs cómmŏn. . . ." These feet are especially striking for the way one crosses over the pause marked by a comma, and next over the even stronger pause marked by a period. These variations slow down (in my own experience) the reading of the line without losing its momentum, for the pauses marked by the comma and period slow the line even as the iambic meter maintains the forward motion. This slowing down encourages a slight lingering over the angels, who will come to play such an important role in the poem's conclusion. The fourth line then slows down to linger on the angels' wings—arguably the poem's key image, for the unfurling of the wings creates the moment of sublime loss—with an anapestic substitution in the second foot: "Ăs lóng | ăs thĕ wíngs | wĕre fúrled, | thĕy félt | nŏ áwe." The addition of this one unstressed syllable is just enough to add a subtle note of emphasis to the image of the wings.

An important idea about prosody that emerges in Justice's work, both his poetry and his critical prose, is that the metrical line functions as the basic material that the poet works with and shapes. By rough analogy—and as Aquinas pointed out long ago, all analogies are rough in one way or another—the verse line is for the poet what color is for the painter, what stone or wood or metal is for the sculptor: the raw material to be formed. One encounters this conception of the verse line in Justice's essay "The Invention of Free Verse" (Justice 1998a, 39–42), which features Ezra Pound in Wabash, Indiana, in 1907, inventing twentieth-century free verse in writing his poem "Cino," tightening up the iambic line by removing unstressed syllables: "if two stresses could be brought together, why not three? From 'Ravens, nights, allurement' only let the slack syllables be dropped," and the experiment yields the line, "Eyes, dreams, lips, and the night goes" ibid., 40; the poem appears in Pound's *Selected Poems* (1956). Thus did the breaking of the iamb open the verse line for further experimentation.

"Children Walking Home from School through Good Neighborhood" (from *The Sunset Maker*; CP 205), which concerns how the techniques of art and other artifice provide ways of experiencing and understanding the world, is an especially interesting case of Justice's handling of the verse line. While the poem employs metrical substitutions as a way of achieving emphasis, it also marks its progression of imagery and thinking by the interplay of regular and irregular lines. Save for the opening line—"Thĕy áre | lĭke fíg | urĕs héld | ĭn sóme | glăss báll"—which establishes the basic iambic meter, the few instances of lines or half-lines that scan as perfect iambs punctuate the movements of the poem; the other lines are made irregular mostly by the substitution of anapests for iambs, one or two per line.

Having established the children as figures in a glass "in which, when shaken, snowstorms occur," the imagery shifts to the children making their way "Oŭt ălóng | thĭs wálk | wăy bĕtwéen | twŏ wórlds," with its two anapestic substitutions. The opening lines establish a comparison of these children as figures in a snow globe making their way across a bridge, which in its swaying becomes a figure of their precarious crossing toward adulthood. Line six then signals the end of this movement of imagery with its run of three perfect iambs: "Thĭs ál | mŏst swáy | ĭňg brídge." Again, it is the relatively rare metrically regular lines, rather than those that carry substitutions, that signal the most conspicuous rhetorical effects by indicating the close of a major image or metaphor.

The three lines that follow further illustrate this rhetorical function of the metrically regular lines:

Ŏctó | bĕr sún | lĭght chéck |ĕrs thĕir páth;
Ĭt fréts | thĕir chéeks | aňd băre árms nów | wĭth shádŏw
Ălmóst | tŏo púre | tŏ síg | nĭf ý | ĭtsélf.

The first two of these lines develop the imagery of light and shadow; the first ends with an anapest, and the second carries a double iamb (for I hear the words *arms* and *now* just edging out *bare*, thus relegating the latter to a relatively unaccented position) and an iamb followed by an extra unstressed syllable. The third line begins with a rather unusual case. The way that I have marked the first foot does not accord wholly with the dictionary's pronunciation for the word *almost*, for the primary pronunciation puts the stress on the first syllable; at the same time, the dictionary (*Webster's Third New International Dictionary*) indicates that a secondary pronunciation does in fact place the stress on the second syllable. It may be that my ear allows the first foot as an iamb largely because—the predominantly iambic rhythm of the poem having been well established at this point—the momentum of this rhythm moves the opening word into its acceptable secondary pronunciation. As this last line quoted scans as perfect iambic pentameter, it also marks the close of the light-and-shadow imagery.

The poem then takes up the musical suggestion of the word *frets*, to develop a metaphor of the children's interaction: "polyphonic voices" that create "short-lived harmonies." The metrical stress here is on the movement of their voices: "vói | cĕs thăt crísscróss." Because of the way that the two syllables of the word *crisscross* drown out the two relatively weak syllables preceding them, I hear feet two and three as a double iamb, leaving the first syllable of *voices* as a defective foot. The final, short line of this section—the iambic trimeter "Ĭn shórt- | lĭved hár | mŏníes"—signals the closure of both the musical metaphor and the first verse paragraph.

After the first verse paragraph, with its multiple frameworks and comparisons (the snow globe, the "almost swaying bridge," sunlight, and music), orients the reader to the scene, the second takes up a more focused and circumstantial description:

> Today, a few stragglers.
> One, a girl, stands there with hands spaced out, so—
> A gesture in a story. Someone's . . .

I find the second of these lines to be the most metrically enigmatic of the poem. One way to scan it is to hear the first syllable as a stand-alone stress (sometimes referred to as a defective foot) followed by an iamb, a trochee, an iamb, and then three syllables that remain quite puzzling. Here is one way that the line might be scanned: "Ŏne, ă gírl, stánds thĕre wĭth hánds spáced ŏut, só." However one might resolve the scansion of the line, the point remains that its irregularity calls an extra measure of attention to these details of the young girl's gesture of story, thus emphasizing the speaker's interest not just in the imagery of the scene, but also in its meaning for these children. The line calls attention to the children's own struggles to understand their world by telling stories. Or rather, the line stresses what the speaker presumes to be these children's struggles, for the run of comparisons and frameworks of the opening paragraph emphasizes the speaker's self-conscious separation from them—hence his conspicuous attempts to understand them. The poem thus delivers a vision of double consciousness: the speaker aware of his struggles to understand the children's experience of the world, as well as their attempts to understand the world and themselves. He sees them walking in the midst of sunlight and the music of their own existence, but at the same time existing in a world that is enclosed, as in "some glass ball," and precarious, as on an "almost swaying bridge."

After this metrically ambiguous line, which strikingly maintains the rhythm that it threatens to derail, the poem returns to its meter with four perfect iambs—"Ă gés | tŭre ín | ă stó | rўّ. Sóme | ŏne's . . . "—ending with the first syllable of *Someone's*, which leads into the anecdote. The iambic tetrameter of this opening portion of the line leads into the speaker's own gesture of story about one of the children's notebooks spilling and the group's dash to pick up the spilled contents. This brief fragment is just enough to suggest the undoing of security in the children's world—no disaster, but a hint of complications to come. What is to come is, in fact, the preoccupation of the closing lines:

> Not that they would shrink or hold back from what may come,
> For now they all at once run to meet it, a little swirl of colors,

Lĭke thĕ léaves | ălréad | ў́ blá | zĭng ańd fál | lĭng fár | thĕr nórth.

The "it" toward which the children run remains ambiguous, though it is legitimate to read the pronoun as referring to "what may come," which associates with "a little swirl of colors," a phrase that may be read in this instance as referring (most immediately) to the leaves "falling farther north" or (just as credibly) to the running children. It requires no great leap of imagination to read these falling leaves as images of the death toward which the children inevitably (as mortals) run. The association of the "little swirl of colors" with both the children and the imagery of death establishes an intimate relationship that the children cannot escape. That the leaves are falling in the North while the children are in the South makes the destination of death remote, though no less real. Themselves a swirl of colors, they run toward the distant colors suggestive of their deaths to come. The poem emphasizes the beauty in the moment of sheer ephemerality, an understanding that is primarily the speaker's, for it is his language that discloses the precariousness of the otherwise commonplace moment.

Unlike the endings of the other sections or movements of this poem, the final line does not resolve into complete metrical regularity; it carries two anapestic substitutions, in the first and fourth feet. These substitutions place stress on the images of leaves and falling, both of which are crucial to the poem's associations that are lightly suggestive of death. At the same time, the lack of resolution back to the metrical regularity that marks earlier movements emphasizes the poem's open-endedness. Here is where the artistic framework leaves off. The earlier moments of metrical regularity, occupying in each case either a whole line or a grammatically isolated partial line, punctuate the movements of the speaker's imagination, which is helpful in understanding the children's lives up to a point. But then, it is only in imagination that he achieves the poem's partial closures. When it comes to the open-endedness of the unpredictable life narratives of the children whom the speaker observes, the poem refuses easy closure, and only gestures toward the final closure on which all may agree.

A poem that appears in the "New Poems" section of *Collected Poems*, "At the Young Composers' Concert" (274), emphasizes how works of art enable one to perceive and understand the world, including the experiences and lifeworlds of other people. This poem stresses that, far from being able to perceive and understand the world innocently, without presupposition or mediation, humans are utterly dependent on art and artifice to enter into an experience of the world. Entering the disciplines of an artistic tradition means entering vast stores of human experience and understanding. If, as Robert K. Logan says, a word "packs a great deal of experience into a single utterance or sign" (45), then such a work of art as a poem packs an astonishing level of experience into a single work. A signal moment concerning this issue in Justice's prose occurs where he emphasizes, in his essay on Philip Larkin's poem "Coming," that the iambic pentameter line "comes trailing" its "tradition and precedent" (1998a, 115). One may fairly expand this statement to mean also that a formal discipline with such a deep history as the iambic pentameter line carries its own store of echoes, knowledge, and experience. Were a young student to delve attentively into the iambic pentameter practices of, say, Chaucer, Shakespeare, Milton, Pope, Wordsworth, and Stevens, it would be difficult for him or her to turn a hand to this line and not feel something of the tragicomic weight of human experience that has been encoded in and carried by it. Even if the young poet working in English were to choose to resist all of these associations (or as many of them as possible), they would continue to exert their influence, in large part precisely as that which the poet resists. In fact, some resistance is necessary if the writer is to avoid simply repeating the past. One benefits from the very tradition, with its accumulation of experiences, that must be resisted.

I propose that similar statements about the accumulation of human experience also hold true about such nonverbal arts as painting and music, whose works are also "strange attractors" (Logan 2007, 45) of experience. The accumulation in art of human experience is a dominant theme of "At the Young Composers' Concert," which begins simply enough:

The melancholy of these young composers
Impresses me. There will be time for joy.

The conversational tone almost successfully conceals the meter, which nevertheless makes itself heard, though gently, lending the weight of the meter's dignity and precedent to the relatively plain statement. The poem then turns its attention to *this* young composer, signaling the turn with the transitional word *meanwhile*, which also constitutes the poem's first metrical substitution, a trochee in the first foot: "Méanwhĭle, | ŏne cán't | hĕlp nó | tĭ cíng | thĕ bóy." After the opening foot, the line maintains the iambic meter against its own odds. Part of the tension—the creation of variations within the established rhythm—arises from the demotion of the monosyllable "help" to the position of an unaccented syllable by the strong first syllable of "noticing," which just successfully edges out the previous word. Further, although one might be tempted to read the second foot as a trochee, at this point of the poem the dominant meter is sufficiently well established to allow "can't" to edge out "one" for the accent. The rhythmic variations of this line, along with the opening substitution, call attention to the speaker's opening reflections on the moment in which the novice composer is bending to the physical instrument of his art as both the focal point and source of feeling:

> Meanwhile, one can't help noticing the boy
> Who bends down to his violin as if
>
> To comfort it in its precocious grief.

It is by responding to the musical instrument's demands that he begins reaching toward his artistic maturity. The feeling encoded by artistic tradition in the physical instrument trigger's the young composer's response. In this moment the violin functions in a way similar to T. S. Eliot's notion of the objective correlative: a "set of objects, a situation, a chain of events which shall be the formula of that particular emotion; such that when the external facts, which must terminate in sensory experience, are given, the emotion is immediately evoked" (1960, 124–25). At the young composers' concert, it is the violin itself that initially functions as the objective correlative, encoding arrays of human emotion that are evoked when the young artist bends to the instrument.

Or rather, that the violin functions as a kind of objective correlative is the speaker's interpretation of the scene. The basic situation of the poem, similar to that in "Children Walking Home from School through Good Neighborhood," is of the speaker trying to understand the experience of another. In thus interpreting the young composer's feeling, the speaker—whom I take to be a version of Justice himself, who was both a composer and a musician —reveals the way in which the whole scene of the concert represents his own feeling for the art. He sees the scene as disclosive of the tradition's dynamics of encoding experience:

> It is his composition, confused and sad,
>
> Made out of feelings he has not yet had
> But only caught some hint or rumor of
>
> In the old scores—and that has been enough.

Perhaps inescapably, the composition is confused, for the composer is in the early stages of accomplishment; but at the same time his study of the old scores has been enough to prevent his composition from becoming *mere* confusion. His confusion has, in other words, been composed by the old scores, which have provided the vicarious experience out of which the young composer has written his work. They function, along with the violin, as objective correlatives of the experiences encoded in artistic tradition. The formal education of music is one of the ways that such experience is passed along. The young composer has been able to access these stores of experience and therefore even bring "feelings he has not yet had" into his work. But the process is not automatic, for it is the rigors of his art that allow him to catch the "hint or rumor" of these feelings; he must practice the art assiduously to take on its store of experience.

The poem then articulates a principle of exceeding technique by means of technique:

And not that we are awed, exactly; still,

There is something *to* this beyond mere adult skill.

The word *still*—which receives emphasis by the variation created as the foot crosses over the pause marked by the semicolon—signals a shift in the speaker's thinking, from the admission that the performance is not awe-inspiring back to the terms of appreciation. The following line, which points out that for all its technical predictability, the piece gets at something unpredictable and marvelous, receives emphasis as the line of the poem that carries the most substitutions, three in all: *anapest*—iamb—*anapest*—*double iamb* (though the last of these counts as two feet). In pushing against the poem's iambic meter, the line threatens to lose the rhythm without doing so, thus stressing the line's statement about exceeding the exigencies of "mere adult skill." This line then prepares the way for the counterintuitive statement that the performance "is the more moving just because it fails." There is a remote echo here of the closing moment in "The Wall," for both poems recount a glimpse of something grand in a moment of failure. Here the speaker realizes that although he is listening to the work of an amateur, he is hearing something more than amateur work. As Longinus emphasized in *On Great Writing*, grandeur can exist in the midst of technical failures.

The final poem of Justice's *Collected Poems*, "There is a gold light in certain old paintings" (278), contemplates in its three sections relationships to four art forms: painting, poetry and music, and drama. As in the two poems just discussed, "There is a gold light" emphasizes the deepening of human experience both through art, the forms of artifice and artificiality that constitute culture, and through involvement with artistic community. This kind of community, centered on attentiveness to and concern with art, helps one to experience the world more profoundly. As the poem progresses, the speaker addresses a virtual artistic community and enters more fully into the art that he contemplates, thereby extending and deepening his own experience and understanding of the world.

In the opening stanza, the speaker remains objectively distanced in his ekphrasis of a crucifixion scene. At the same time, there is a communal gesture in the plural pronoun when he describes the light "like happiness, when we are happy." The statement implies that the speaker is looking at the painting with a group. The poem forms a virtual gathering—composed of whoever reads the text—to contemplate a virtual painting. It also implies involvement with the artwork insofar as one's mood at the time of viewing influences how one interprets the light. Viewing the painting—however distanced one's stance—also means enough of an entry into the scene to lend one's own affect to the light. Further, the line implicitly appeals to the universality of attributing to the painting one's own mood, thus reading it in sympathy with one's own emotional state.

In the second stanza, the speaker becomes more conspicuously a part of the artistic community concerned with Orpheus, along with the art he describes: "We think he sang then, but the song is lost." Here the virtual community, signaled again by *we,* expands beyond the viewers of the previous stanza's painting to include the community that through the centuries has concerned and connected itself with the Orpheus myth. This community includes such tellers of the tale of Orpheus and Eurydice as Virgil (*Georgics,* Book Four) and Ovid (*Metamorphoses,* Book Ten), both of whom tell the Orpheus story but of course do not disclose the song. Virgil, for example, recounts that

> Through seven months he wept alone beneath
> A cliff and lofty caves, beside the Strymon's
> Waters, unraveling his tale in song
> That charmed the tigers and drove the oaks to move.

As Mark Jarman has pointed out, the important figure of Orpheus in Justice's poems is connected especially with the arts of poetry and music, the two arts that come to the fore in this stanza of "There is a gold light," for both are implied in the Latin word *carmen,* which I have translated in the passage above as "song." Included in this section also is the tradition of poetry that has given us the Orpheus story. Just as the pursuit of these arts is an "endeavor of the living" (Jarman 2001, 92), so also this pursuit connects one with those artists of the past who have kept the tradition alive for the present day. At the end of this stanza, the speaker enters more fully into the scene by making his claim about Orpheus's song: "I say the song went this way: *O prolong / Now the sorrow if that is all there is to prolong.*" Here Justice does what neither Virgil nor Ovid dares: he provides a version of the mythic poet's song.

The final stanza prolongs the sorrow by envisioning a better future that is indefinitely deferred. Justice achieves this deferral by entering into Chekhov's play *Uncle Vanya*, speaking through the persona of Sonya addressing the title character in her final speech. Gone from Justice's version, though, is any vision of a heavenly realm that would make the idealized version possible. He provides instead a vision of a future that the poem holds out no hope will ever come to pass. This version of the speech differs strikingly from that in Chekhov's play, which begins, "We shall work for the sake of others, now and when we are old, never knowing peace or rest." Sonya then seeks refuge in her vision of heavenly reward: "And you and I, my dear Uncle Vanya, we shall see a life which is bright, beautiful, and fine. We shall rejoice and look back on our present misfortunes with a feeling of tenderness, with a smile—and we shall rest. . . . We shall see all these earthly evils, all our sufferings, drowned in mercy that will fill the whole world, and our life will then grow quiet and gentle and sweet as a caress" (95). Justice's version begins with the stark terms, "The world is very dusty, Uncle. Let us work." He then echoes other details from Sonya's speech, and ends by associating human existence with suffering:

The orchard will bloom; someone will play the guitar.
Our work will be seen as strong and clean and good.
   And all that we suffered through having existed
   Shall be forgotten as though it had never existed.

Human existence and suffering are especially strongly linked in the second-to-last line. Much depends on what one relates most strongly to the word *through*. As I read the line, the word wavers in its association, from "suffered through" to "through having existed." Reading it the former way makes the line mean something like, "Having existed, we of course suffered." Reading it the latter way makes the line mean, "We suffered in our existence." The two meanings overlap considerably; together, they stress the link between suffering and existence more powerfully.

These lines bring to closure both the poem and Justice's *Collected Poems*. This concluding poem maps an increasingly intimate and circumstantial involvement with art, until in these final lines the speaker of the poem melds with one of Chekhov's characters. After the detached description of a rendering of the Cross that Justice found compelling as art but not as doctrine, the poem's speaker melds with the figure of Orpheus singing his lines about the prolongation of sorrow. Returning from his journey to the underworld, which is also his sojourn in the arts of music and myth, the speaker returns to a vision the everyday world as blooming, dusty, and difficult. And yet, he returns to this difficult world with the Orphic lines that the underworld has yielded. He returns to a difficult world transformed by art; even if the world is the same, the speaker himself is transformed.

The Orpheus section of "There is a gold light" signals Justice's long engagement with the story of the mythic poet. In "In Memory of Orpheus," Mark Jarman notes Justice's affinities with the Orpheus myth, the "story of an artist's excellence and loss" (2001, 84), as well as the parallel between Justice's work as an elegist and Orpheus's descent into the underworld in search of Eurydice, for in his elegies Justice goes in search of what is lost. As an Orphic poet of communion with the dead, Justice stands in a lineage with the Wordsworth of Kurt Fosso's *Buried Communities: Wordsworth and the Bonds of Mourning* (2004), which explores the Romantic poet's work as a formation of communities that include both the living and the dead. One of the model poems of this dynamic is Wordsworth's "We Are Seven," about an encounter with a "little cottage girl" who confounds the poem's speaker by insisting that she and her siblings comprise seven, even though two of them have died. She makes a habit of going to her dead siblings' graves, singing to them, and eating in their company, for her community extends beyond the grave (see Fosso 4–5, 128–29). As Fosso points out, in Wordsworth "it is not community that leads to a connection to the dead so much as it is the dead, and more specifically the relationship of the living to them, that leads to community" (7). Community includes the living and the dead and is formed by remembrance of them: telling their stories, constructing and interpreting commemorative monuments, observing traditional and improvised rituals—what Fosso refers to as the "fundamental rites of neighborhood" (175).

With regard to this inclusive sense of community, Wordsworth's poetry looks to the figure of Orpheus, whose story he translated from Virgil's *Georgics* (Fosso 31). In this story of his double loss of Eurydice, Orpheus exemplifies an "open-eyed refusal to negate or replace the dead"; he acknowledges "loss while resisting all mediating symbolic substitutes" (ibid., 32). He refuses to negate Eurydice or to allow a substitute that would relieve his grieving; rather, he gives voice to and draws out his mourning for what is permanently lost. As Justice has him sing in "There is a gold light," "*O Prolong / Now the sorrow if that is all there is to prolong."* One of the great fears of the grief-stricken is not that sorrow will continue, but that it will cease, taking with it memory of the dead, as if they had never existed. As the mythic figure of endless mourning, Orpheus offers assurance of the persistence of memory and implied communion—by means of memory—with the dead. He turns his endless mourning into art that itself assures that those in the grave will be remembered by the living.

Justice stands as a latter-day Orphic poet in the sense of one who communes with the dead. Among his elegiac poems that I have already discussed are "On the Death of Friends in Childhood," "Tales from a Family Album," "Homage to the Memory of Wallace Stevens," "Sonatina in Yellow," "First Death," "Thinking about the Past," and "The Sunset Maker." Often, Justice's elegiac speakers stand in isolation, though "On the Death of Friends in Childhood" uses the first-person plural and addresses the personification of memory. Many of the elegies, though, point toward the emergence of a community gathered by memory of the dead. "Homage to the Memory of Wallace Stevens," for example, addresses Stevens directly, but it also implicitly includes Milton by means of the echo of the closing line of "Lycidas," and similarly included are the readers who care about this tradition as Justice does. Although his elegies include a variety of people—for instance, his father in "Sonatina in Yellow"; his grandmother in "First Death"; Eleanor, "Mary Something," Margery, Benton, and Kenny in "Thinking about the Past"; his mother in "Psalm and Lament"—I focus here primarily on literary community, which includes not only poets and other writers, but also anyone attentive to literary tradition.

An early poem of communion with the dead and with the literary past is "The Return of Alcestis" (CP 52), which appeared in *The Old Bachelor and Other Poems* (1951) and Justice's 1954 doctoral dissertation at Iowa but was not included in his major books until the *Selected Poems* of 1979. While he made alterations to the poem in its various printings, by the time of the *Collected Poems* he had changed it all back to the 1951 version, save for the archaic touch of "hath" in the closing line:

HERCULES: I bring Alcestis from the dolorous shades.

ADMETUS: Ah, what can ail her, that she weeps nor smiles.

ALCESTIS: My latest sighs have somewhat scorched the veil.
Ah, what can ail me, that I weep nor smile?
Why hath he brought me from the dolorous shades?

The story of Alcestis has a long literary history, going back at least as far as Euripides' play, in which the title character agrees to die in place of her husband, Admetus. Hercules, a guest in Admetus's house, having unknowingly violated the proper observances for the role of a guest in a house of mourning, brings Alcestis back from the land of the dead. Chaucer, in *Legend of Good Women*, has Alcestis assign the poet the task of writing the *Legend*. Milton, in "Sonnet 23," also makes use of the myth:

> Methought I saw my late espoused saint
> > Brought to me like Alcestis from the grave,
> > Whom Jove's great son to her glad husband gave,
> > Rescued from Death by force, though pale and faint.

The Alcestis myth, in its various manifestations, tends to carry along with it an ambivalent attitude toward the return of the beloved, which brings complications into the world of the living. In the Milton sonnet, for example, the forced rescue from death, leaving Alcestis "pale and faint," remains a mixed blessing; and the comparison of the speaker's vision of his "late espoused saint" to Alcestis implies a similarly complex attitude toward his dream. Alcestis's melancholy return to the living signals that the past cannot be fully restored, but rather experienced only as a "pale and faint" version of itself. In Euripides, Admetus speaks of his desire to do what he cannot—journey to the underworld to rescue his wife:

> If I had the song and poetry of Orpheus
> so I could charm the god of Hell, bewitch his queen
> and, by my singing, spell you back from death,
> I'd go beneath the ground. (51)

The reference to Orpheus here is disruptive, since bringing his wife back from the dead is the precise endeavor at which Orpheus fails. Even after Hercules restores Alcestis to the living, she must remain silent until "three days have passed,/and the bitter stain of death has disappeared" (93). But this stain does not disappear within the text of the play, which ends with Alcestis in silent thrall to the gods below, not yet participating fully in the world of the living, her restoration promised but deferred, the sorrow prolonged.

Justice's Alcestis fragment, with its notes of memory and loss, anticipates much of the complicated tone of his later work. Even though Alcestis has been freed from the "dolorous shades," she weeps and does not smile, nor does she understand what troubles her even as she finds herself restored to her husband. The fragment's final question registers some ambivalence about this restoration, even as the penultimate question signals confusion at her lack of joy. Her sighs have "somewhat scorched" though not burned through the veil that separates the living from the dead. Given where the poem leaves off, with its unfulfilled anticipation, the idea emerges that one's debts to the gods of the dead—and by implication the gods of the past—cannot be paid.

As befits this state of indebtedness, Justice's comic prose poem "Orpheus Opens His Morning Mail" (CP 65) begins with the mythic poet sorting through "Bills. Bills." The debts to the past accumulate. Ironically, this portrait of Orpheus no longer lamenting or longing for Eurydice is pathetic in a way that the figure of him prolonging his sorrow is not. When he laments Eurydice, the pathos of the scene never descends into the pitiable, for in uttering his lamentation he is also an artist in the strength of his form. The only mention of Eurydice in the prose poem is the note that he receives for her, marked "Please Forward." It is not so much that regaining her is deferred, but that he has given up either seeking or grieving her. His song is therefore silenced, and we are left only with a portrait of the artist in quotidian retirement.

The long middle paragraph describes a world of adulation for the speaker, which is now in the past tense. Even though he receives a "group photograph, signed: *Your Admirers*," he pictures the "rooms into which they must once have locked themselves to read my work." The phrasing of his speculation about where "they must *once* have" (emphasis mine) read his work emphasizes his feeling that his moment is past. Further, the scenes in which he pictures them—like the figures in the photograph, dressed in costumes "at once transparent and identical, like those of young ladies at some debauched seminary"—come with the commonplace trappings of decadence: "ostentatiously unmade" beds, a "pinched chrysanthemum." A pall of exhaustion, of a cultural moment dying of lethargy, falls over the scene. The poet himself cries out, "O lassitudes!" Even in the final paragraph—which holds out the possibility of something new, "an invitation to attend certain rites," where he is to be guest of honor—a certain sameness settles in: "As always, I rehearse the scene in advance: the dark; the guards, tipsy as usual, sonorously snoring." But then he is forced to confront his own state of mind: "But O my visions, my vertigoes! Have I imagined it only, the perverse gentility of their shrieks?" Having given up his mourning, Orpheus has given up his community as well. Even if his admirers, along with their shrieks, exist wholly in the world after all, and not merely in his imagination, this genteel and culturally lethargic community hardly befits the artist's former stature.

This portrait of the disengaged artist contrasts sharply with the personal engagement of "For the Suicides of 1962" (CP 96–97). The permutations of the dedication disclose something of the poem's historical bases, though there may be mysteries here that will never be solved (and this is among the most mysterious of Justice's poems). In the original edition of *Night Light*, where the poem is titled "For the Suicides of 1962," the dedication reads "In Memory: J & G." In the 1982 revised edition of *Night Light*, where the title is shortened to "The Suicides," another initial is added to the dedication: "In Memory: J & G & G." Jean Justice believes that this extra "G" was a misprint, and that the accurate dedication is what appears in the 1979 *Selected Poems*: "in memory of J. and G. and J."[1] She recalls that one of these "J's" refers to John Berryman, who did not commit suicide until 1972, after the original printing of the poem but well before the extra "J" was added to the dedication in the revised *Night Light*. The three letters of this latter dedication also make up the version that appears in *A Donald Justice Reader* (1991) and *New and Selected Poems* (1995)—where the title becomes "For the Suicides." However, the dedication is shortened again to "in memory: J & G" in the British selected poems, *Orpheus Hesitated beside the Black River* (1998), and *Collected Poems* (2004); and in both of these cases, the title of the poem is restored to "For the Suicides of 1962."

Justice seems to have taken some artistic license when he added the dedication to Berryman after the poem was already written, as well as in his use of the year 1962 in the title. Further, of the three instances of suicide recounted in the poem—by drowning, shooting, and hanging—it is the first that seems apt to Berryman, though he committed suicide by jumping off a bridge over the Mississippi River, rather than into a bay (as in the poem), and his body landed near a pier and rolled down an embankment, meaning that the cause of death was not drowning (Haffenden 419). I will maintain the anonymity of the other victims of suicide, though I specify that one was a fiction writer and the other the spouse of a student at the Writers' Workshop; thus, each has some connection to Justice's literary community. Of the three suicides recounted in the poem, the description of the last is arguably the most disquieting:

> deep within the black
> Forest of childhood that tree
>
> Was already rising which,
> With the length of your body,
> Would cast the double shadow.

Justice sometimes spoke of someone he knew hanging herself near the family Christmas tree—therefore the double shadow. In each case the death to come takes on a cast of fate: the bay "preparing herself" to receive one; the pistol "slowly learning to flower" in the hands of another; the tree growing in the "Forest of childhood" of the last. The image of the third, with its double shadow, may be taken to represent what has shadowed all three of these lives.

What precisely this shadowing something is remains undisclosed. Conspicuously even among Justice's poems of restraint, this one keeps its secrets. On the one hand, there is the point that the speaker takes from these deaths: "we did not care for you/Nearly enough." Might it be this neglect that has shadowed them? On the other hand, the poem constantly hints at more that never emerges fully into the speaker's utterance. He recalls—or rather "we recall," for there is a community formed here by remembrance of the dead—softened voices that "must have drifted back/ /A long way to have reached us"; and the dead have entered a "labyrinth" while the living can only stand "at the threshold,/ /Peering in." Perhaps the poem's most puzzling lines are those that precede the final section:

> At the end of your shadow
> There sat another, waiting,
> Whose back was always to us.

Is this figure death? the cast of fate? tragic circumstances? The poem maintains its silence on the question.

Without resolving the mystery into clear sense, the final two quatrains bring a sense of closure by purely artistic means, reinforced by the repeating end words that form mirror images of each other:

> When the last door had been closed,
> You watched, inwardly raging,
> For the first glimpse of your selves
> Approaching, jangling their keys.
>
> Musicians of the black keys,
> At last you compose yourselves.
> We hear the music raging
> Under the lids we have closed.

The very selves of the dead have become depersonalized, for these "selves" approach the dead, "jangling their keys," as if they are others. This sense of alienation is to be expected, for the "masks by which we knew you/Have been torn from you." Even if the shedding of the masks hints at some gesture of authenticity, it was the masks—now torn away—by which "we" knew them. How shall we know them without the familiar masks? Nevertheless, these dead do finally manage to "compose" themselves in an act of artistic accomplishment. They are musicians of the melancholy black keys that make music "Under the lids" of the coffins that have become their instruments. The turn to music is important here for its abstraction—as the speaker of "The Sunset Maker" says, alluding to Stravinsky, music must be abstract "to be music" (CP 235). These "Musicians of the black keys" have composed themselves without disclosing what their compositions mean. Community is formed here not only by remembering the dead and taking the point that their deaths have made about neglect, but also by standing before and honoring the mystery they have composed.

Justice further extends his literary community into the land of the dead in his poem "Hell" (CP 214), in which "R. B. Vaughn speaks." In his essay "Oblivion: Variations on a Theme," Justice connects his old friend with the poet Ser Brunetto (who had been something of a mentor to Dante) in Canto 15 of The Inferno (1998a, 68). As the persona of Justice's poem, Vaughn speaks in terms of his belatedly Romantic yearnings: "After so many years of pursuing the ideal / I came home." The ideal remains elusive, something glimpsed "in the blue-silver wake / Of island schooners, bound for Anegada, say," that is, in the constant flux of the water in the schooner's wake—an image of movement always, like the schooner, going elsewhere. Or again, the ideal may be seen flickering in "torches by the railroad tracks in Medellín." The flickering of these torches provides an image of the constant movement within which the ideal can only be glimpsed, as the flames represent such passion as this ideal inspires. Perhaps the most poignant of the ideal's representations is the rose that the speaker once fantasized would resolve all ambiguities:

> When I was very young I thought that love would come
> And seize and take me south and I would see the rose;
> And that all ambiguities we knew would merge
> Like orchids on a word. Say this:
> I sought the immortal word.

In articulating the ideal of all ambiguities resolving in the image of the single rose, the poem moves back into multiplicity as the rose gives way to the plural "orchids." Further, the poem itself already frustrates the resolution of ambiguity as it becomes unclear whether the command "Say this" means that the speaker would have the addressee refer to him ("[He] sought the immortal word") or quote him verbatim. And even if the addressee does in fact quote the line "I sought the immortal word," will this "I" refer to the addressee-turned-speaker, or perhaps to a role he is playing at his friend's request? Or perhaps both of these possibilities are to resolve into a single meaning, as the role becomes the addressee's identity. The poem signals that this final resolution in the "immortal word" will not come to pass; the unified ideal is encountered only in the dispersal of its fragments, articulated by the multiple voices of its devotees.

Justice includes something of Vaughn's voice in this poem. As his note to the poem points out, line six ("In torches by the railroad tracks in Medellín") "is taken unchanged from 'The Spell,' a poem in Robert Boardman Vaughn's unpublished ms."[2] Further, parts of the "next few lines are freely adapted from another poem of his, 'The Black Rose'" (CP 281). In chapter 1 I quoted a version of "The Black Rose" that Vaughn enclosed in a letter to Justice; here I quote from the version that appears in the unpublished manuscript in my possession:

> When I was very young I thought that Love
> Would seize her creature like a great white bird
> And take him South to see stone roses,
> Talk with Gordon Pym among the ashes settling there.
> But that's before I learned the war of wills,
> The care and resolution
> Of the ambiguities that stalk my every line
> And merge like orchids on the word.

By bringing Vaughn's voice into his text, Justice brings himself into literary communion with his dead poet friend.

He also pays tribute to his friend with "In Memory of the Unknown Poet, Robert Boardman Vaughn" (CP 213). As emphasized in chapter 1, Justice saw Vaughn's life as tragically aimed. In this villanelle he commemorates the accordance of Vaughn's life to Eliot's dictum of seeing "beneath both beauty and ugliness" to "the boredom, and the horror, and the glory" (1933, 98). In recalling Vaughn's bohemian and itinerant life, the poem also recounts the way that Justice believed his friend may have died:

> Probably at the end he was not yet sorry,
> Even as the boots were brutalizing him in the alley.

Again, in his essay "Oblivion: Variations on a Theme," Justice recounted the rumors that reached him of Vaughn's death:

Later, I heard that he had been beaten to death in the hallway of a halfway
house in Manhattan; later still, that the beating had taken place instead in an
alley running alongside the halfway house. All versions were plausible enough,
but I believed this last one. It was winter when I heard it, and I remembered
those alleys from our early days together in the city. [Remember that they
shared a New York apartment as young men.] It was easy to picture such
an alley with the cold winds barreling through, and patches of snow crusted
between the knocked-over and spilling ash cans. (1998a, 64)

Justice uses this imagined scene in the villanelle:

I picture the snow as falling without hurry
To cover the cobbles and the toppled ashcans completely.

Even before his death, Vaughn is already "half a spirit," on his way to becoming the shade who will speak in Justice's "Hell." However, the closing notes
of the villanelle call attention to Vaughn's fierce and inspiring devotion to
the art of poetry:

But I remember the fiery
Hypnotic eye and the raised voice blazing with poetry.

Here Vaughn's appearance echoes the "flashing eyes" of the dread-inducing,
holy poet at the end of Coleridge's "Kubla Khan." In Justice's virtual community of artists, Vaughn is the model not of discipline, but of complete
devotion, even abandonment, to artistic pursuit.

As noted earlier, in his essay on Justice, Laurence Donovan reflects, "I
believe that Don records in his writings the passing of a time and place that
were truly unique, and that bred a type of American now disappearing from
the scene" (CS 109). From the available evidence, I suspect that this "type"
is a person "of remarkable talent and interest" (ibid.) who pursues his or her
art with great devotion and independently of any promise of a career. Justice
tended to speak highly of such people—John Lenox, for example (see chapter
1). He paid tribute to Carl Ruggles as "one of those gifted amateurs of the
arts that America produced, especially in the early modern period—Marsden
Hartley and Charles Burchfield among the painters, Charles Ives and Roy
Harris among the composers, and Sherwood Anderson, perhaps Hart Crane,
among the writers" (2001, 25). Justice's earlier image of himself seemed to
conform to such a portrait. He conjectured that back when he was teaching
at the University of Miami, he must have "figured I would go on meeting
freshman composition classes till I was old and grey, by which time I would
have become a good poet, with plenty of money from the novels I would

have been writing. Something like that" (ibid., 34–35). Striking about this fantasy is that the novel writing was conceived as a way of supporting the poetry rather than a career in itself. That he could make a living as a professor of poetry writing must have come as a surprise.

His tribute to John Lenox came in the form of "In Memory of My Friend, the Bassoonist, John Lenox" (CP 211–12). Unlike Vaughn, Lenox was a model of discipline and stability, for "Lonely/ / In eminence he sat, Like some lost island king." Overlooking the bay where he keeps his boat, he pursues his interests, as evidenced by the

> silver flute
> He taught himself to play,
> Casually, one evening.

He is thus an "autodidact supreme." This singular devotion contrasts with the speaker's depiction of the contemporary scene, which has caused Lenox's "high porch" to go "up in the smoke of money, money"—the pursuit of such worldly success as Laurence Donovan protests. In the midst of his diatribe, though, the speaker pulls himself up short:

> The barbarians . . .
> > But enough.
> You are missed. Across the way,
> Someone is practicing sonatas,
> And the sea air smells again of good gin.

He interrupts his rant at precisely the moment that it threatens to violate the art of the poem, which has more to do with recalling Lenox's life and addressing him now that he is dead than with declaiming a jeremiad against the contemporary scene. He pictures Lenox as part of an ideal artistic community:

> No, you are off somewhere,
>
> Off with Gauguin and Christian
> Amid hibiscus'd isles.

In addressing Lenox directly, the speaker momentarily enters this community as well, and the recollection of Lenox leads to a recognition that even in the midst of the "booboiseries of the neighbors" (Mencken must also be a member of this community; see 560, n. 1), the life of art continues, for someone "is practicing sonatas," even if it is across the way. And as Jarman indicates (2001, 87), the smell of good gin is better than that of bad.

"The Artist Orpheus" (CP 240), a sonnet first collected in *New and Se-lected Poems*, offers quite a different version of the mythic poet from the earlier "Orpheus Opens His Morning Mail." In it, the poet remains actively engaged with his art, on which his journey to the land of the dead remains focused; nevertheless, the story of Eurydice is only alluded to, and then only *as* a story. What the artist seems to be seeking in the underworld is the past, especially his own earlier years: "Childhood came blazing back at him." Several of the poem's details accommodate the underworld to the everyday human life-world; thus, the landscape is "much like Florida's," and when Orpheus plays music, he plays Ravel. It would be difficult to miss the reference to the state of Justice's birth, or miss the relevance of Ravel to his interest in music; this underworld corresponds with the world of the poet's memory. As the figure of the poet travels into the world of memory, his present image fades:

> They glided across a black
> And apathetic river which reflected nothing back
> Except his own face sinking gradually from view
> As in a fading photograph.

To cross into the underworld, they would have to cross the River Styx, though the Lethe-like effects of this river contribute to the artist's self-forgetfulness —a version of the depersonalization that, for Justice, successful art demands. As Orpheus plays Ravel and there are tears in Hell for the first time, the self-forgetfulness pervades the whole scene as all are taken into the moment: "Years passed, or a day." This is not the mythic time out of time, for tem-porality still exists. Rather, this is a moment—whatever its clock duration might be—of absorption in the temporality of the music; it is temporality made into art.

At first the turn into the sestet seems about to lead into the Eurydice story: "And the shades relented finally and seemed sorry." However, by the next line, Eurydice is already lost, and the story is put into question:

> He could have sworn then he did not look back,
> That no one had been following on his track,
> Only the thing was it made a better story
> To say that he had heard a sigh perhaps
> And once or twice the sound a twig makes when it snaps.

If he is correct that "no one had been following on his track," then it seems that Eurydice—who is never named in the poem—was never there to be-gin with. This artist is devoted to telling the tale, so that the sigh and the snapping twig—hints that someone might be following—are included in the telling because they make a "better story." The accomplishment of the verse narrative is what matters on this journey.

Another poem focused on the accomplishment of verse is "Invitation to a Ghost" (CP 245), in which the major emphases of this present chapter—commemoration and direct address of the dead leading to a community dedicated to art—converge. The poem is dedicated to Henri Coulette (1927–88), Justice's classmate from the Writers' Workshop, whose *Collected Poems* (1990) he edited with Robert Mezey. The invitation is an occasion of literary community, as the speaker welcomes Coulette's ghost to the gathering:

> Sit with us. Let it be as it was in those days
> When alcohol brought our tongues the first sweet foretaste of oblivion.

This "foretaste of oblivion" is of course the effect of the alcohol, but it is difficult to encounter the word *oblivion* in this context and not to think of Justice's article of that title (1998a, 52–68)—in which he commemorates Kees, Coulette, and Vaughn, recognizing the varying levels of oblivion to which they have gone—or of the darkness that memories rise from and fall back into in "Thinking about the Past." The implied gathering that the poem alludes to is dedicated to confronting such oblivion as memories rise from and sink into, with the idea that this work of memory can fix something of the past into place in artistic terms. This gathering is concerned specifically with the art of poetry:

> And what should we speak of but verse? For who would speak of such
>   things now but among friends?
> (A bad line, an atrocious line, could make you wince: we have all seen it.)

People who knew Justice will recognize here a description of his own response to anything he found distasteful, certainly including atrocious lines of verse. The existence of this artistic community also explains why the poet calls out, "Come back now and help me with these verses." Recall that it was Coulette whom Berryman called on first to comment on Justice's sonnet, later titled "The Wall." This speaker seeks to allow moments of the past to make their fine impressions.

Fittingly, this poem about a gathering of the living and the dead includes a treatment of the Orpheus and Eurydice myth:

> Correct me if I remember it badly,
> But was there not a dream, sweet but also terrible,
> In which Eurydice, strangely, preceded *you?*

And you followed, knowing exactly what to expect, and of course she did
turn.

As Jarman has pointed out (2001, 91), Coulette is here cast in the roles of
both Orpheus and Eurydice at once. Given that he is coupled with Eurydice,
Coulette is by implication Orpheus. At the same time, given the implied
narrative—that he is following the other out of the underworld—he is in the
traditional role of Eurydice. As a member of this literary community of both
the living and the dead, Coulette is both in the role of the living poet and in
that of the friend residing in the underworld. Justice takes on his own version of the role of Orpheus, recovering his memory of Coulette, a memory
that is bound to fade—a memory that is already in question: "Correct me
if I remember it badly." But even if the memory fails, there is the poem to
prolong the sorrow, "if that is all there is to prolong" (in the words of "There
is a gold light"); prolonging the sorrow means also prolonging at least some
residue of the memory.

As in "The Artist Orpheus," the underworld here is memory, for when the
poet asks for some secret, it is a recollection not from the land of the dead,
but rather from that of the living: "Whisper to me some beautiful secret that
you remember from life." A secret worth knowing must come from life, but
which one might have missed. In Justice's poetry life in this world is what
we have, for there is no hereafter. The secrets that we can discern are those
that we seek with memory in the shadows.

In the summer of 1995, Donald and Jean took a trip to England with their longtime friend Robert Mezey, to visit Thomas Hardy country. Mezey recalls their visit to the house that Hardy designed for Emma and himself: "We went out to Max Gate on a beautiful sunny afternoon and walked around the grounds, examining the pet cemetery and 'the Druid Stone' (of 'The Shadow on the Stone') and the many trees Hardy had planted."[1] The "Druid Stone" is a slab that was discovered while digging the house's foundation (Millgate 258). As the visitors were walking around the grounds, the couple living at Max Gate as tenants and caretakers invited them into the house. "We sat and drank tea and talked with them for a long time and eventually they took us on a tour of the whole house, including Hardy's study and the little room upstairs where Emma died and so much more."[2] In this way they joined the "parade of teatime visitors" (ibid., 525) reaching back to the days when the Hardys themselves lived at Max Gate. What was this gathering for tea but an observance of the "rites of neighborhood" (Fosso 175) in honor of Thomas and Emma Hardy?

Donald had retired from the University of Florida in May 1992, and he and Jean returned to Iowa City. Along with continuing his writing during these years, he was also painting and composing music. His paintings have appeared in several places. For example, they grace the front and back covers of an issue of *Solo*, a poetry journal edited by Glenna Luschei, who refers to Justice as her "teacher and hero" (III); and they appear on the covers of several of Justice's later books, including *Collected Poems*. From July 15 to October 15, 1999, his paintings were on display at the Yager Museum in Oneonta, New York, along with work by Elizabeth Bishop, Mark Strand, and Derek Walcott.[3] Some of Justice's musical compositions were publicly performed. His piece "Sunday Afternoons"—a setting for an excerpt from his poem "Nostalgia and Complaint of the Grandparents"—was performed at Clapp Recital Hall in Iowa City by the Iowa Community String Orchestra in 2001.

During his last years he struggled with his health. As his obituary in the *New York Times* (August 10, 2004) recounts, the Library of Congress offered him the position of Poet Laureate in 2003, but health issues forced him to decline. He had Parkinson's disease and died of pneumonia on the morning of August 6, 2004, less than a week before his seventy-ninth birthday and fewer than two weeks before the release of *Collected Poems*. At just under three hundred pages, the volume is much shorter than the life's work of many poets, but the relatively slender output is more than offset by the consistent quality. It is not that all of the poems are equal, but rather that one can count on them never to fall below a very high standard. In this regard he stands alongside such figures as T. S. Eliot and Elizabeth Bishop.

In describing Justice's stature, David Orr (writing in the *New York Times Book Review*) said that in the "world of American poetry, Donald Justice wasn't a bit player; he was an Olivier." I believe that Justice, a lover of movies, would have appreciated the cinematic metaphor, though his favorite actors were John Wayne and Cary Grant. The differences between these very different acting styles—the earthy and the elegant—signal the complexity of Justice's sensibility and style, and connect with his commitment to experimentation. From the start he did not want to keep repeating the same thing; he devoted himself to variety.

At the same time, an understanding of one's own moment and where it might be going requires a critical understanding of the past. As Orr wrote of Justice's interest in nostalgia, "It's as if, by looking determinedly backward, he looked further ahead than almost anyone else." He resisted the facile patterns of interpretation whereby history becomes either a steady progress or an ongoing process of decay. If his poems disclose a world in fragments, they also put into question whether it has ever been otherwise. They show a world that has always been in certain states of decay while it has also been constantly under construction, like those "buildings and archways to forever unfinished subdivisions" that Jean Justice writes existed in the Miami of Donald's childhood (5). But the world still delivers its moments of wonder:

> Turn your head. Look. The light is turning yellow.
> The river seems enriched thereby, not to say deepened.
> Why this is, I'll never be able to tell you.
>
> ("Villanelle at Sundown," CP 215)

If we imagine a gold or silver age at the cost of simplistic fantasy, there are nevertheless glimpses of something that strains if not exceeds description.

As set out in chapter 2, "The Wall" delivers Justice's poems into the ambiguous history that he went on to explore throughout his life. Toward the end of his life he was writing poems that took up historical figures, such as "A Man of 1794" (about Robespierre) and "The Voice of Col. von Stauffenberg Ascending through the Smoke and Dull Flames of Purgatory" (whose title character was part of a plot to assassinate Hitler). Many of these later, historical poems take place in the Great Depression of Justice's childhood, though not from the child's point of view. Among these are "Mule Team and Poster" (after a photograph by Walker Evans, 1936), "Cinema and Ballad of the Great Depression," "Banjo Dog Variations," and "Pantoum of the Great Depression." In the second of these, the speaker, having described the difficulty of his and his friends' circumstances, ends on a note of qualified, even strained, optimism:

> Things will go better one day, boys.
> Don't ask when.
> *A decade hence, a war away.*
> O meet me in the Red Star Mission then!
>
> Pulled out an ancient mouth harp and began to play. (CP 219)

Justice well knows that there is no guarantee that things will get better, as the line "Don't ask when" indicates. There may be many years and the tragedy of a war before change occurs. In the meantime, there is the Red Star Mission and the pursuit of art, as the harmonica implies.

One reason that art of whatever kind is called for is that there are few if any guarantees. As "Pantoum of the Great Depression" (CP 260–61) points out, life in history, unlike in art, has no careful plotting. The poem is laden with terms from Aristotle's *Poetics: tragedy, heroic, chorus, verse, pities and fears, audience, flaws, virtues, poetry.* The poem resists the relevance of these terms to everyday life, sometimes quite ironically: "Thank god no one said anything in verse"—the speaker, of course, uses iambic pentameter in uttering his thanks that no one spoke in verse. Similarly, the closing lines deny the relevance of art: "But it is by blind chance only that we escape tragedy. / / And there is no plot in that; it is devoid of poetry." But poetry can have an uncanny power even as it denies its own relevance. At times, art can be quite irrelevant, and we have art to remind us of as much.

Justice maintained deep convictions about life and art, but he was also constantly asking further questions. He was a pluralist in the best sense: that of knowing that there is no single adequate perspective, theoretical or artistic, to reveal all of the complications and nuances of actuality. He pursued a variety of approaches to illuminate different parts of ourselves and our world, without trying to set these approaches into a singular, overarching view. He has left us with a body of work that continues to disclose its secrets remembered from life.

Chapter 1. Artistic Vocation

1 Dana Gioia, "Tradition and an Individual Talent," in *Certain Solitudes*, ed. Gioia and Logan, 77; hereafter cited in the text as CS.

2 Justice, *Collected Poems*, 239, hereafter cited in the text as CP.

3 Justice, "An Interview with David Hamilton and Lowell Edwin Folsom," in *Platonic Scripts*, 101; hereafter cited in the text as PS.

4 Personal conversation with the author, 19 February 2001. Conversations between Donald Justice and the author occurred over a period of years during the late 1990s and early 2000s.

5 Telephone conversation with Jean Justice, 12 August 2005. Many of the details of this paragraph come also from Jean Justice's "Tales from a Family Album: The Justices."

6 Personal conversation with the author.

7 Personal conversation with the author.

8 E-mail from Donald Justice, 11 October 2001.

9 Quoted in Richard Stern, "Donald Justice: A Small Portrait in Letters," unpublished essay supplied to the author by Stern.

10 Ibid.

11 Personal conversation with the author.

12 Personal conversation with the author.

13 Donald Justice to Barbara Pearson, 19 October 1946. This letter was in the possession of Jean Justice; other letters written by Donald Justice that were consulted for this book are in the Paul Engle papers, University of Iowa Library, Special Collections, Iowa City, Iowa.

14 The letter is undated; the envelope is postmarked 17 July 1958.

15 In Justice 2001, Justice gives the date of the conference as 1948. Jean (Ross) Justice recalls that she and Donald attended the conference in both 1947 and 1948. Although Donald, in the interview with Hoy, evidently places all of his recollections of this conference in 1948, surely some of these events—such as the interactions with Robert Penn Warren—belong in 1947. According to Joseph Blotner's biography, Warren was in Italy in 1948, but Blotner places Warren in Greensboro, North Carolina, in spring 1947 (231–49).

16 E-mail from Jean Justice, 21 June 2005.

17 Personal conversation, summer 2003.

18 Jean Justice, personal conversation, November 2001.

19 The details of this paragraph come from conversations with Donald and Jean Justice over a period of years.

20 The details of this paragraph come from a conversation with Donald Justice during the summer of 2003.

21 Donald Justice to Paul Engle, 3 May 1953.

22 Telephone conversation with Jean Justice, 12 August 2005.

23 Conversation with Donald Justice.

24 Telephone interview with Ronald (Rocco) DiLorenzo, 9 June 2007.

25 Marvin Bell, e-mail dated 27 July 2003.

26 Donald Justice to Paul Engle, 14 February 1956.

27 Donald Justice to Paul Engle, 26 May 1956.

28 Donald Justice to Paul Engle, 14 June 1957.

29 From Robert Boardman Vaughn's unpublished manuscript *Boreen*, in the author's possession.

30 Robert Vaughn to Donald Justice, 24 August 1959, courtesy of Jean Justice.

31 Robert Vaughn to Donald Justice, 18 October 1959, courtesy of Jean Justice.

Chapter 2. Solemn Vows

1 Translations of Dante are my own.

2 E-mail from Jean Justice, 23 January 2007.

3 I would include in this select group "On the Death of Friends in Childhood," "The Wall," "The Missing Person," "Poem," "Children Walking Home from School through Good Neighborhood," "Villanelle at Sundown," and "There is a gold light in certain old paintings."

4 E-mail from Jean Justice, 23 January 2007.

5 Translations of Virgil are my own.

Chapter 3. Missing Selves

1 E-mail, 27 June 2008.

2 Ibid.

3 Donald Justice to Paul Engle, 5 November 1964.

4 Donald Justice to Paul Engle, 28 December 1964.

5 E-mail from Jean Justice, 3 August 2007.

6 Donald Justice to Paul Engle, 13 May 1965.

7 Personal conversations during the 1990s and 2000s.

8 Donald Justice to Paul Engle, 13 May 1965.

9 E-mail from Jean Justice, 5 August 2007.

10 I owe thanks to my students for helping me develop my understanding of this poem: Adam Bartling, Jessica Cartwright, Henry Chanin, Anna Crandall, Stephen Forbush, Jacob Kraus, Emma Pelkey, Danny Schiff, and Ahmed Yusuf.

11 Despite my consultation with several MacDonald readers, I have not been able to track down the precise source of this quotation.

12 On more than one occasion Justice spoke to me about his interest in this book.
13 For the sake of clarity, I identify this person by his code name "Gilbert" (in quotation marks) and refer to Gilbert Norman by first and last name without quotation marks.
14 Shakespeare references are to act, scene, and line.

Chapter 4. Not Addressed to You

1 Personal conversation.
2 E-mail from Jean Justice, 5 July 2005.

Chapter 5. Artistic Disclosures

1 Justice told me this story in the late 1990s or early in the 2000s.
2 Heaney offered this explanation as part of a reading he gave at the University of Iowa, Iowa City, Iowa, 14 May 1996.
3 Letter to the author, 27 August 1991.

Chapter 6. Orpheus in After Time

1 Jean Justice and I exchanged a series of e-mails about this issue in August 2008.
2 I do not find this poem, or the line, in the unpublished manuscript of Vaughn's, titled *Boreen*, in my possession.

Conclusion

1 E-mail from Robert Mezey, 25 October 2005.
2 Ibid.
3 The installation was titled "Poems without Words, The Visual Artwork of Poets: Elizabeth Bishop, Donald Justice, Mark Strand, Derek Walcott."

Abrams, M. H. (1971). *Natural Supernaturalism: Tradition and Revolution in Romantic Literature*. New York: W. W. Norton.

Aeschylus. (1975). *The Oresteia: Agamemnon, The Libation Bearers, The Eumenides*. Trans. Robert Fagles. Introduction by Robert Fagles and W. B. Stanford. New York: Penguin Books.

Alexander, Hubert H. (2001). *Peter Taylor: A Writer's Life*. Baton Rouge: Louisiana State University Press.

Allen, Donald M., ed. (1960). *The New American Poetry*. New York: Grove Press.

Aristotle. (1984). *The Complete Works of Aristotle*. Revised Oxford translation. Vol. 2. Ed. Jonathan Barnes. Princeton, N.J.: Princeton University Press.

Arnold, Matthew. (1965). *Culture and Anarchy with Friendship's Garland and Some Literary Essays*. Ed. R. H. Super. Ann Arbor: University of Michigan Press.

Atkins, Elizabeth. (1936). *Edna St. Vincent Millay and Her Times*. Chicago: University of Chicago Press.

Auden, W. H. (1991). *Collected Poems*. Ed. Edward Mendelson. New York: Vintage Books. Corrected from 1976 edition.

Augustine. (1960). *The Confessions of St. Augustine*. Trans. John K. Ryan. New York: Image Books.

Barnes, Hazel E. (1997). *The Story I Tell Myself: A Venture in Existentialist Autobiography*. Chicago: University of Chicago Press.

Barrett, William. (1958). *Irrational Man: A Study in Existentialist Thought*. New York: Doubleday.

Bate, Walter Jackson. (1970). *The Burden of the Past and the English Poet*. Cambridge, Mass.: Belknap Press of Harvard University Press.

Beach, Christopher. (2003). *The Cambridge Introduction to Twentieth-Century American Poetry*. Cambridge: Cambridge University Press.

Bentley, Eric. (1953). *In Search of Theater*. New York: Alfred A. Knopf.

Bishop, Elizabeth. (1979). *The Complete Poems 1927–1979*. New York: Farrar, Straus and Giroux.

Bloom, Harold. (1973). *The Anxiety of Influence: A Theory of Poetry*. New York: Oxford University Press.

———. (1976). *Wallace Stevens: The Poems of Our Climate*. Ithaca, N.Y.: Cornell University Press.

———. (1987). An Interview with Imre Salusinszky. In *Criticism in Society*. New York: Methuen.

———. (2003). *A Map of Misreading*. New York: Oxford University Press. First published 1975.

Blotner, Joseph. (1997). *Robert Penn Warren: A Biography*. New York: Random House.

Blumenberg, Hans. (1993). "Light as a Metaphor for Truth: At the Preliminary Stage of Philosophical Concept Formation." Trans. Joel Anderson. In *Modernity and the Hegemony of Vision*, ed. David Michael Levin. Berkeley: University of California Press, 30–62.

Bourjaily, Vance. (1964). *The Hound of Earth*. New York: Dial Press. First published 1955.

Boym, Svetlana. (2001). *The Future of Nostalgia*. New York: Basic Books.

Brooks, Cleanth. (1985). "A Tribute to Richard Eberhart." *South Atlantic Quarterly* 50:4, 21–33.

Brooks, Cleanth, and Robert Penn Warren. (1960). *Understanding Poetry*. 3rd ed. New York: Holt, Rinehart and Winston. First published 1938.

Bruns, Gerald L. (1980). "Anapostrophe: Rhetorical Meditations upon Donald Justice's 'Poem.'" *Missouri Review* 4:1.

Bürger, Peter. (1984). *Theory of the Avant-Garde*. Trans. Michael Shaw. Minneapolis: University of Minnesota Press.

Burgess, Geoffrey, and Bruce Haynes. *The Oboe*. New Haven, Conn.: Yale University Press, 2004.

Burke, Edmund. (1998). *A Philosophical Enquiry into the Sublime and the Beautiful and Other Pre-Revolutionary Writings*. Ed. David Womersley. New York: Penguin Books. First published 1757.

Chekhov, Anton. (1977). *Anton Chekhov's Plays*. Trans. Eugene K. Bristow. New York: W. W. Norton.

Conrad, Joseph. (2003). *Under Western Eyes*. Oxford: Oxford University Press. First published 1911.

———. (2004). *The Secret Agent: A Simple Tale*. New York: Modern Library. First published 1907.

Cotkin, George. (2003). *Existential America*. Baltimore, Md.: Johns Hopkins University Press.

Coulette, Henri. (1966). *The War of the Secret Agents and Other Poems*. New York: Charles Scribner's Sons.

———. (1990). *The Collected Poems of Henri Coulette*. Ed. Donald Justice and Robert Mezey. Fayetteville: University of Arkansas Press.

Dana, Robert, ed. (1991). *What I Think I Know: New and Selected Poems*. Chicago: Another Chicago Press.

Dante Alighieri. (2003). *The Inferno*. Trans. Henry Wadsworth Longfellow. Intro. Peter Bondanella. New York: Barnes and Noble Classics.

Derrida, Jacques. (1997). *Of Grammatology*. Trans. Gayatri Chakravorty Spivak. Baltimore, Md.: Johns Hopkins University Press. Corrected from 1976 edition.

Dickinson, Emily. (1999). *The Poems of Emily Dickinson*. Ed. R. W. Franklin. Reading Edition. Cambridge, Mass.: Belknap Press of Harvard University Press.

Donceel, Joseph. (1979). *The Searching Mind: An Introduction to a Philosophy of God.* Notre Dame, Ind.: University of Notre Dame Press.

Eberhart, Richard. (1936). *Reading the Spirit.* London: Chatto and Windus.

Eichenberg, Fritz. (1983). *Dance of Death: A Graphic Commentary on the Danse Macabre through the Centuries.* New York: Abbeville Press.

Eliade, Mircea. (1954). *The Myth of the Eternal Return: or, Cosmos and History.* Trans. Willard R. Trask. Princeton, N.J.: Princeton University Press. First published 1949 as *Le Mythe l'éternel retour: archétypes et répétition.*

Eliot, T. S. (1933). *The Use of Poetry and the Use of Criticism: Studies in the Relation of Criticism to Poetry in England.* Cambridge, Mass.: Harvard University Press.

———. (1960). *Selected Essays.* New ed. New York: Harcourt, Brace and World.

———. (1962). *Collected Poems 1909-1962.* New York: Harcourt, Brace and World.

Erasmus, Desiderius. (2003). *The Praise of Folly.* 2nd ed. Trans. Clarence H. Miller. New Haven, Conn.: Yale Nota Bene/Yale University Press.

Euripides. (1974). *Alcestis.* Trans. William Arrowsmith. New York: Oxford University Press.

Faulkner, William. (1961). *Three Famous Short Novels.* New York: Vintage Books.

———. (1964). *Absalom, Absalom!* New York: Modern Library.

Ferlazzo, Paul J. (1976). *Emily Dickinson.* Boston: Twayne.

Fosso, Kurt. (2004). *Buried Communities: Wordsworth and the Bonds of Mourning.* New York: State University of New York Press.

Frazer, William, and John J. Guthrie, Jr. (1995). *The Florida Land Boom: Speculation, Money, and the Banks.* Westport, Conn.: Quorum Books.

Freud, Sigmund. (2003). *The Uncanny.* Trans. David McLintock. New York: Penguin Books. First published 1919.

Frizell, Bernard. (1946). "Existentialism." *Life* 20:24 (June), 59-66.

Fuller, Jean Overton. (1958). *Double Webs: Light on the Secret Agents' War in France.* London: Putnam.

Fulton, Ann. (1999). *Apostles of Sartre: Existentialism in America, 1945-1963.* Evanston, Ill.: Northwestern University Press.

Gioia, Dana, and William Logan, eds. (1997). *Certain Solitudes: On the Poetry of Donald Justice.* Fayetteville: University of Arkansas Press.

Grene, Marjorie. (1959). *Introduction to Existentialism.* Chicago: University of Chicago Press.

Haffenden, John. (1983). *The Life of John Berryman.* London: Ark Paperbacks. First published 1982.

Hamilton, Ian. (1982). *Robert Lowell: A Biography.* New York: Random House.

Harp, Jerry. (1999). "Fidelities to Form." *The Iowa Review* 29:3, 167-72.

Hassan, Ihab. (1971). *The Dismemberment of Orpheus: Toward a Postmodern Literature.* New York: Oxford University Press.

Heaney, Seamus. (2001). *Electric Light.* New York: Farrar, Straus and Giroux.

Hepburn, Allan. (2005). *Intrigue: Espionage and Culture.* New Haven, Conn.: Yale University Press.

Homer. (1974). *The Iliad*. Trans. Robert Fitzgerald. New York: Anchor Books.

Hudgins, Andrew. (2002). "Homage: Donald Justice." *Southern Review* 38:3, 654–61.

Iser, Wolfgang. (1980). "The Reading Process: A Phenomenological Approach." In *Reader-Response Criticism: From Formalism to Post-Structuralism*. Baltimore, Md.: Johns Hopkins University Press, 50–69.

Izzo, David Garrett. (2002). *The Writings of Richard Stern: The Education of an Intellectual Everyman*. Jefferson, N.C.: McFarland.

James, Henry. (1924). *The Turn of the Screw; The Two Magics: The Turn of the Screw, Covering End*. New York: Macmillan.

Jarman, Mark. (1984). "Ironic Elegies: The Poetry of Donald Justice." *Pequod: A Journal of Contemporary Literature and Contemporary Criticism* 16–17 (1980), 104–9.

———. (2001). "In Memory of Orpheus: Three Elegies by Donald Justice." In *The Secret of Poetry*. Ashland, Ore.: Story Line Press.

———. (2002). "Happiness: The Aesthetics of Donald Justice. *Blackbird* (fall): http://www.blackbird.vcu.edu/v1n2/nonfiction/jarman_m/justice.htm.

Johnson, Samuel. (1861). *Lives of the Most Eminent English Poets, with Critical Observations on Their Works*. Vol. 1. New York: Derby and Jackson.

———. (1977). *Samuel Johnson: Selected Poetry and Prose*. Ed. Frank Brady and W. K. Wimsatt. Berkeley: University of California Press.

Jonson, Ben. (1974). *Ben Jonson's Conversations with William Drummond of Hawthornden*. Ed. R. F. Patterson. New York: Haskell House.

Justice, Donald. (1943). "The Scarred Men, She." *Mademoiselle* (February): 180.

———. (1951). *The Old Bachelor and Other Poems*. Miami: Pandanus Press.

———. (1958). "San Francisco and Palo Alto." *Western Review* 22:3, 231–34.

———. (1960). *The Summer Anniversaries*. Middletown, Conn.: Wesleyan University Press. Revised edition published 1981.

———, ed. (1962). *The Collected Poems of Weldon Kees*. Lincoln: University of Nebraska Press. First issued 1960 as a limited edition from Stone Wall Press, Iowa City.

———. (1967). *Night Light*. Middletown, Conn.: Wesleyan University Press. Revised edition published 1981.

———. (1973). *Departures*. New York: Atheneum.

———. (1979). *Selected Poems*. New York: Atheneum.

———. (1984). *Platonic Scripts*. Ann Arbor: University of Michigan Press.

———. (1987). *The Sunset Maker: Poems/Stories/A Memoir*. New York: Atheneum.

———. (1991). *A Donald Justice Reader: Selected Poetry and Prose*. Hanover, N.H.: Middlebury College Press/University Press of New England.

———. (1995). *New and Selected Poems*. New York: Alfred A. Knopf.

———. (1998a). *Oblivion: On Writers and Writing*. Ashland, Ore.: Story Line Press.

———. (1998b). "Death, Night, Etc." *Yale Review* 86:2, 63–75.

———. (1998c). *Orpheus Hesitated beside the Black River: Poems 1952–1997*. London: Anvil Press.

———. (1999). "A Miranda's World." In *A Community of Writers: Paul Engle and the Iowa Writers' Workshop*. Ed. Robert Dana. Iowa City: University of Iowa Press.

————. (2001). *Donald Justice in Conversation with Philip Hoy*. London: Between the Lines.

————. (2003). Foreword to *Dog Island and Other Florida Poems*, Laurence Donovan. Sarasota, Fla.: Pineapple Press.

————. (2004). *Collected Poems*. New York: Alfred A. Knopf.

Justice, Jean Ross. (2007). "Tales from a Family Album: The Justices." *The Iowa Review* 37:1, 1–12.

Kafka, Franz. (1952). *Selected Short Stories*. Trans. Willa and Edwin Muir. New York: Modern Library.

Kant, Immanuel. (1960). *Observations on the Feeling of the Beautiful and the Sublime*. Trans. John T. Goldthwait. Berkeley: University of California Press. First published 1764.

Kant, Immanuel. (2007). *Critique of Judgement*. Trans. James Creed Meredith and Nicholas Walker. Oxford: Oxford University Press. First published 1790.

Kirwan, James. (2005). *Sublimity: The Non-Rational and the Irrational in the History of Aesthetics*. New York: Routledge.

Lacan, Jacques. (2002). *Écrits: A Selection*. Trans. Bruce Fink with Héloïse Fink and Russell Grigg. New York: W. W. Norton.

Lehman, David. (1998). *The Last Avant-Garde: The Making of the New York School of Poets*. New York: Doubleday.

Logan, Robert K. (2007). *The Extended Mind: The Emergence of Language, the Human Mind, and Culture*. Toronto: University of Toronto Press.

Logan, William. (2005). "Poetry Chronicle: The Great American Desert." *New Criterion* (June), 66–73.

Longinus. (1991). *On Great Writing (On the Sublime)*. Trans. G. M. A. Grube. Indianapolis, Ind.: Hackett.

Luschei, Glenna. (2001). "Publisher's Foreword." *Solo* 4, III.

Lyotard, Jean-François. (1989). "The Sublime and the Avant-Garde." In *The Lyotard Reader*, ed. Andrew Benjamin. Cambridge, Mass.: Basil Blackwell, 196–211.

McGann, Jerome J. (1991). *The Textual Condition*. Princeton, N.J.: Princeton University Press.

McLuhan, Marshall H. (1962). *The Gutenberg Galaxy: The Making of Typographic Man*. Toronto: University of Toronto Press.

Mariani, Paul. (1996). *Dream Song: The Life of John Berryman*. 2nd ed. Amherst: University of Massachusetts Press. First published 1996.

Masereel, Frans. (1942). *Danse Macabre*. New York: Pantheon Books.

Mencken. H. L. (1937). *The American Language: An Inquiry into the Development of English in the United States*. New York: Alfred A. Knopf.

Miller, J. Hillis. (1985). *The Linguistic Moment: From Wordsworth to Stevens*. Princeton, N.J.: Princeton University Press.

————. (1991). *Theory Now and Then*. Durham, N.C.: Duke University Press.

————. (2002). *On Literature*. New York: Routledge.

Millgate, Michael. (1982). *Thomas Hardy: A Biography*. New York: Random House.

Milton, John. (1998). *The Riverside Milton*. Ed. Roy Flannagan. New York: Houghton Mifflin.

Nadeau, Maurice. (1965). *The History of Surrealism*. Trans. Richard Howard. New York: Macmillan.

Ong, Walter J. (1977). *Interfaces of the Word: Studies in the Evolution of Consciousness and Culture*. Ithaca, N.Y.: Cornell University Press.

——. (1982). *Orality and Literacy: The Technologizing of the Word*. New York: Routledge.

——. (1986). *Hopkins, the Self, and God*. Toronto: University of Toronto Press.

Orr, David. (2004). "The Ironist of Nostalgia" (A review of Justice's *Collected Poems*). *New York Times*. (29 August). Accessed online at http://query.nytimes.com.

Ovid. (1970). *Metamorphoses*. Trans. Arthur Golding. Ed. Madeleine Forey. Baltimore, Md.: Johns Hopkins University Press.

Percy, Walker. (1983). *Lost in the Cosmos: The Last Self-Help Book*. New York: Washington Square Press.

Perkins, David. (1987). *A History of Modern Poetry: Modernism and After*. Cambridge, Mass.: Belknap Press of Harvard University Press.

Perloff, Marjorie. (2003). *The Vienna Paradox: A Memoir*. New York: New Directions.

Pope, Alexander. (1963). *The Poems of Alexander Pope*. New Haven, Conn.: Yale University Press.

Postman, Neil. (1985). *Amusing Ourselves to Death: Public Discourse in the Age of Show Business*. New York: Penguin Books.

Pound, Ezra. (1934). "The Teacher's Mission." *English Journal* 23:8 (October), 630–35.

——. (1956). *Selected Poems*. New York: New Directions.

Rahner, Karl, and Herbert Vorgrimler. (1965). *Theological Dictionary*. Ed. Cornelius Ernst, O.P. Trans. Richard Strachan. New York: Herder and Herder.

Ransom, John Crowe. (1968). *The World's Body*. Baton Rouge: Louisiana State University Press. First published 1938.

Reidel, James. (2003). *Vanished Act: The Life and Work of Weldon Kees*. Lincoln: University of Nebraska Press.

Reiss, Timothy J. (1982). *The Discourse of Modernism*. Ithaca, N.Y.: Cornell University Press.

Revill, David. (1992). *The Roaring Silence: John Cage: A Life*. New York: Arcade.

Roache, Joel. (1971). *Richard Eberhart: The Progress of an American Poet*. New York: Oxford University Press.

Ryle, Martin, and Kate Soper. (2002). *To Relish the Sublime? Culture and Self-Realization in Postmodern Times*. New York: Verso.

Sacks, Peter. (1985). *The English Elegy: Studies in the Genre from Spenser to Yeats*. Baltimore, Md.: Johns Hopkins University Press.

Sartre Jean-Paul. (1944). "The Republic of Silence." *Atlantic Monthly* 174:6 (December), 39–40.

——. (1956). *Being and Nothingness: A Phenomenological Essay on Ontology*. Trans.

Hazel E. Barnes. New York: Washington Square Press. First published in French 1943.

———. (1964). *Nausea*. Trans. Lloyd Alexander. New York: New Directions. First published in French 1938.

Shakespeare, William. (1982). *Hamlet*. Ed. Harold Jenkins. The Arden Edition of the Works of William Shakespeare. London: Methuen.

———. (2001). *The Sonnets*. Ed. Stephen Orgel. New York: Penguin Books.

———. (1999). *The Tempest*. Ed. Virginia Mason Vaughan and Alden T. Vaughan. The Arden Edition of the Works of William Shakespeare. London: Methuen.

Shapiro, Alan. (1993). "The New Formalism." In *In Praise of the Impure, Poetry and the Ethical Imagination: Essays, 1980–1991*. Evanston, Ill.: Tri Quarterly Books, 61–76.

Simic, Charles. (2006). "The Memory Piano" (review of *Collected Poems* by Donald Justice). In *The Memory Piano*. Ann Arbor: University of Michigan Press, 225–36.

Spiegelman, Willard. (2004). "Poetry in Review" (review of Donald Justice's *Collected Poems*). *Yale Review* 92:4 (October), 157–73.

Stern, Richard. (1981). *The Chaleur Network*. Sagaponack, N.Y.: Second Chance Press. First published as *In Any Case*. New York: McGraw-Hill, 1962.

Stevens, Wallace. (1957). *Opus Posthumous*. Ed. Samuel French Morse. New York: Alfred A. Knopf.

———. (1987). *The Collected Poems*. New York: Alfred A. Knopf, 1987.

Stewart, Garrett. (1996). *Dear Reader: The Conscripted Audience in Nineteenth-Century British Fiction*. Baltimore, Md.: Johns Hopkins University Press.

Strand, Mark. (1970). "Donald Justice." In *Contemporary Poets*. New York: St. Martin's Press.

Symons, Arthur. (1899). *The Symbolist Movement in Literature*. London: William Heinemann.

Thoreau, Henry David. (1965). *Walden or, Life in the Woods and On the Duty of Civil Disobedience*. New York: Harper and Row.

Tompkins, Jane P. (1980). *Reader-Response Criticism: From Formalism to Post-Structuralism*. Baltimore, Md.: Johns Hopkins University Press.

Tracy, David. (1999a). "Fragments: The Spiritual Situation of Our Times." In *God, the Gift, and Postmodernism*. Ed. John D. Caputo and Michael J. Scanlon. Bloomington: Indiana University Press, 170–81.

———. (1999b). "African American Thought: The Discovery of Fragments." *Black Faith and Public Talk: Critical Essays on James H. Cone's "Black Theology and Black Power."* Ed. Dwight N. Hopkins. New York: Orbis Books, 29–38.

Wallace, Robert. (1996). "Meter in English." In *Meter in English: A Critical Engagement*. Ed. David Baker. Fayetteville: University of Arkansas Press, 3–42.

White, Beatrice A. (1931). Introduction. *The Dance of Death*. Ed. Florence Warren. Early English Text Society, No. 181. London: Oxford University Press.

Wilbers, Stephen. (1980). *The Iowa Writers' Workshop: Origins, Emergence, and Growth*. Iowa City: University of Iowa Press.

Wilson, Edmund. (1931). *Axel's Castle: A Study in the Imaginative Literature of 1870–1930*. New York: Macmillan.

Wimsatt, W. K. (1954). *The Verbal Icon: Studies in the Meaning of Poetry*. Lexington: University of Kentucky Press.

Winters, Yvor. (1947). *In Defense of Reason*. Denver: University of Denver Press.

Ziffrin, Marilyn J. (1994). *Carl Ruggles: Composer, Painter, and Storyteller*. Urbana: University of Illinois Press.